BAKING

easy-to-make great home bakes

BAKING

easy-to-make great home bakes

contributing editor:
CAROLE CLEMENTS

TED SMART

This edition produced for
The Book People Ltd
Hall Wood Avenue
Haydock
St Helens WA11 9UL

© Anness Publishing Limited 2002
Hermes House, 88–89 Blackfriars Road, London SE1 8HA

ISBN 1 84309 144 5

Publisher: Joanna Lorenz
Project Editor:Carole Clements
Designer: Sheila Volpe
Photography, styling: Amanda Heywood
Food Styling: Elizabeth Wolf-Cohen, Carla Capalbo,
steps by Cara Hobday, Teresa Goldfinch, Nicola Fowler

Previously published as *The Great Big Baking Book*

Printed and bound in Hong Kong

© Anness Publishing Limited 1994, 1999, 2001
Updated © 2002
1 3 5 7 9 10 8 6 4 2

CONTENTS

~

INTRODUCTION

~

Nothing equals the satisfaction of home baking. No commercial cake mix or shop-bought biscuit can match one that is made from the best fresh ingredients with all the added enjoyment that baking at home provides – the enticing aromas that fill the house and stimulate appetites, the delicious straight-from-the-oven flavour, as well as the pride of having created such wonderful goodies yourself.

The Great Big Baking Book is filled with familiar favourites as well as many other lesser known recipes. Explore the wealth of biscuits, buns, tea breads, yeast breads, pies, tarts, and cakes within these pages. Even if you are a novice baker, the easy-to-follow and clear step-by-step photographs will help you achieve good results. For the more experienced home baker, this book will provide some new recipes to add to your repertoire.

Baking is an exact science and needs to be approached in an ordered way. First read through the recipe from beginning to end. Set out all the required ingredients before you begin. Size 3 eggs are assumed unless specified otherwise, and they should be at room temperature for best results. Sift the flour after you have measured it, and incorporate other dry ingredients as specified in the individual recipes. If you sift the flour from a fair height, it will have more chance to aerate and lighten.

When a recipe calls for folding one ingredient into another, it should be done in a way that incorporates as much air as possible into the mixture. Use either a large metal spoon or a long rubber or plastic scraper. Gently plunge the spoon or scraper deep into the centre of the mixture and, scooping up a large amount of the mixture, fold it over. Turn the bowl slightly so each scoop folds over another part of the mixture.

No two ovens are alike. Buy a reliable oven thermometer and test the temperature of your oven. When possible bake in the centre of the oven where the heat is more likely to be constant. If using a fan-assisted oven, follow the manufacturer's guidelines for baking. Good quality baking tins can improve your results, as they conduct heat more efficiently.

Practice, patience and enthusiasm are the keys to confident and successful baking. The Great Big Baking Book will inspire you to start sifting flour, breaking eggs and stirring up all sorts of delectable homemade treats – all guaranteed to bring great satisfaction to both the baker and those lucky enough to enjoy the results.

BISCUITS & BARS

~

Keep the biscuit tin filled with this wonderful array of biscuits and bars – some soft and chewy, some crunchy and nutty, some rich and sinful, and some plain and wholesome. All are irresistible.

Farmhouse Biscuits

MAKES 18

4 oz (115 g) butter or margarine, at room temperature

3½ oz (100 g) light brown sugar

2½ oz (70 g) crunchy peanut butter

1 egg

2 oz (55 g) plain flour

½ tsp baking powder

½ tsp ground cinnamon

⅛ tsp salt

6 oz (170 g) muesli

2 oz (55 g) raisins

2 oz (55 g) chopped walnuts

1 Preheat a 350°F/180°C/Gas 4 oven. Grease a baking sheet.

2 With an electric mixer, cream the butter or margarine and sugar until light and fluffy. Beat in the peanut butter. Beat in the egg.

3 ▲ Sift the flour, baking powder, cinnamon and salt over the peanut butter mixture and stir to blend. Stir in the muesli, raisins and walnuts. Taste the mixture to see if it needs more sugar, as muesli varies.

4 ▲ Drop rounded tablespoonfuls of the mixture onto the prepared baking sheet about 1 in (2.5 cm) apart. Press gently with the back of a spoon to spread each mound into a circle.

5 Bake until lightly coloured, about 15 minutes. With a metal spatula, transfer to a rack to cool. Store in an airtight container.

Crunchy Oatmeal Biscuits

MAKES 14

6 oz (170 g) butter or margarine, at room temperature

6 oz (170 g) caster sugar

1 egg yolk

6 oz (170 g) plain flour

1 tsp bicarbonate of soda

½ tsp salt

2 oz (55 g) rolled oats

2 oz (55 g) small crunchy nugget cereal

~ **VARIATION** ~

For Nutty Oatmeal Biscuits, substitute an equal quantity of chopped walnuts or pecans for the cereal, and prepare as described.

1 ▲ With an electric mixer, cream the butter or margarine and sugar together until light and fluffy. Mix in the egg yolk.

2 Sift over the flour, bicarbonate of soda and salt, then stir into the butter mixture. Add the oats and cereal and stir to blend. Refrigerate for at least 20 minutes.

3 Preheat a 375°F/190°C/Gas 5 oven. Grease a baking sheet.

4 ▲ Roll the mixture into balls. Place them on the sheet and flatten with the bottom of a floured glass.

5 Bake until golden, 10–12 minutes. With a metal spatula, transfer to a rack to cool completely. Store in an airtight container.

Farmhouse Biscuits (top), Crunchy Oatmeal Biscuits

Oaty Coconut Biscuits

MAKES 48

6 oz (170 g) quick-cooking oats
3 oz (85 g) desiccated coconut
8 oz (225 g) butter or margarine, at room temperature
4 oz (115 g) caster sugar + 2 tbsp
2 oz (55 g) dark brown sugar
2 eggs
4 tbsp milk
1½ tsp vanilla essence
4 oz (115 g) plain flour
½ tsp bicarbonate of soda
½ tsp salt
1 tsp ground cinnamon

1 Preheat a 400°F/200°C/Gas 6 oven. Lightly grease 2 baking sheets.

2 ▲ Spread the oats and coconut on an ungreased baking sheet. Bake until golden brown, 8–10 minutes, stirring occasionally.

3 With an electric mixer, cream the butter or margarine and both sugars until light and fluffy. Beat in the eggs, 1 at a time, then the milk and vanilla. Sift over the dry ingredients and fold in. Stir in the oats and coconut.

4 ▼ Drop spoonfuls of the mixture 1–2 in (2.5–5 cm) apart on the prepared sheets and flatten with the bottom of a greased glass dipped in sugar. Bake until golden, 8–10 minutes. Transfer to a rack to cool.

Crunchy Jumbles

MAKES 36

4 oz (115 g) butter or margarine, at room temperature
8 oz (225 g) caster sugar
1 egg
1 tsp vanilla essence
5 oz (140 g) plain flour
½ tsp bicarbonate of soda
⅛ tsp salt
2 oz (55 g) crisped rice cereal
6 oz (170 g) chocolate chips

~ **VARIATION** ~

For even crunchier biscuits, add 2 oz (55 g) walnuts, coarsely chopped, with the cereal and chocolate chips.

1 Preheat a 350°F/180°C/Gas 4 oven. Lightly grease 2 baking sheets.

2 ▲ With an electric mixer, cream the butter or margarine and sugar until light and fluffy. Beat in the egg and vanilla. Sift over the flour, bicarbonate of soda and salt and fold in carefully.

3 ▼ Add the cereal and chocolate chips. Stir to mix thoroughly.

4 Drop spoonfuls of the mixture 1–2 in (2.5–5 cm) apart on the sheets. Bake until golden, 10–12 minutes. Transfer to a rack to cool.

Oaty Coconut Biscuits (top), Crunchy Jumbles

Ginger Biscuits

MAKES 36

8 oz (225 g) caster sugar

3½ oz (100 g) light brown sugar

4 oz (115 g) butter, at room temperature

4 oz (115 g) margarine, at room temperature

1 egg

3 fl oz (85 ml) black treacle

9 oz (250 g) plain flour

2 tsp ground ginger

½ tsp grated nutmeg

1 tsp ground cinnamon

2 tsp bicarbonate of soda

½ tsp salt

1 Preheat a 325°F/170°F/Gas 3 oven. Line 2–3 baking sheets with greaseproof paper and grease lightly.

2 ▲ With an electric mixer, cream half of the caster sugar, the brown sugar, butter and margarine until light and fluffy. Add the egg and continue beating to blend well. Add the treacle.

3 ▲ Sift the dry ingredients 3 times, then stir into the butter mixture. Refrigerate for 30 minutes.

4 ▲ Place the remaining sugar in a shallow dish. Roll tablespoonfuls of the biscuit mixture into balls, then roll the balls in the sugar to coat.

5 Place the balls 2 in (5 cm) apart on the prepared sheets and flatten slightly. Bake until golden around the edges but soft in the middle, 12–15 minutes. Let stand for 5 minutes before transferring to a rack to cool.

> ~ **VARIATION** ~
>
> To make Gingerbread Men, increase the amount of flour by 1 oz (30 g). Roll out the mixture and cut out shapes with a special cutter. Decorate with icing, if wished.

Orange Biscuits

MAKES 30

4 oz (115 g) butter, at room temperature
7 oz (200 g) sugar
2 egg yolks
1 tablespoon fresh orange juice
grated rind of 1 large orange
7 oz (200 g) plain flour
1 tablespoon cornflour
½ teaspoon salt
1 teaspoon baking powder

1 ▲ With an electric mixer, cream the butter and sugar until light and fluffy. Add the yolks, orange juice and rind, and continue beating to blend. Set aside.

2 In another bowl, sift together the flour, cornflour, salt and baking powder. Add to the butter mixture and stir until it forms a dough.

3 ▲ Wrap the dough in greaseproof paper and refrigerate for 2 hours.

4 Preheat the oven to 375°F/190°C/ Gas 5. Grease 2 baking sheets.

5 ▲ Roll spoonfuls of the dough into balls and place 1–2 in (2.5–5 cm) apart on the prepared sheets.

6 ▼ Press down with a fork to flatten. Bake until golden brown, 8–10 minutes. With a metal palette knife transfer to a rack to cool.

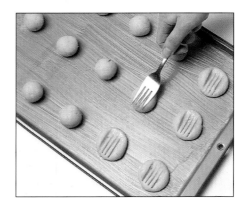

Cinnamon-Coated Cookies

MAKES 30

4 oz (115 g) butter, at room temperature
12 oz (350 g) caster sugar
1 tsp vanilla essence
2 eggs
2 fl oz (65 ml) milk
14 oz (400 g) plain flour
1 tsp bicarbonate of soda
2 oz (55 g) finely chopped walnuts
FOR THE COATING
5 tbsp sugar
2 tbsp ground cinnamon

1 Preheat a 375°F/190°C/Gas 5 oven. Grease 2 baking sheets.

2 With an electric mixer, cream the butter until light. Add the sugar and vanilla and continue mixing until fluffy. Beat in the eggs, then the milk.

3 ▲ Sift the flour and bicarbonate of soda over the butter mixture and stir to blend. Stir in the nuts. Refrigerate for 15 minutes.

4 ▲ For the coating, mix the sugar and cinnamon. Roll tablespoonfuls of the mixture into walnut-size balls. Roll the balls in the sugar mixture. You may need to work in batches.

5 Place 2 in (5 cm) apart on the prepared sheets and flatten slightly. Bake until golden, about 10 minutes. Transfer to a rack to cool.

Chewy Chocolate Biscuits

MAKES 18

4 egg whites
10 oz (285 g) icing sugar
4 oz (115 g) cocoa powder
2 tbsp plain flour
1 tsp instant coffee
1 tbsp water
4 oz (115 g) finely chopped walnuts

1 Preheat a 350°F/180°C/Gas 4 oven. Line 2 baking sheets with greaseproof paper and grease the paper.

~ **VARIATION** ~

If wished, add 3 oz (85 g) chocolate chips to the mixture with the nuts.

2 With an electric mixer, beat the egg whites until frothy.

3 ▼ Sift the sugar, cocoa, flour and coffee into the whites. Add the water and continue beating on low speed to blend, then on high for a few minutes until the mixture thickens. With a rubber spatula, fold in the walnuts.

4 ▲ Place generous spoonfuls of the mixture 1 in (2.5 cm) apart on the prepared sheets. Bake until firm and cracked on top but soft on the inside, 12–15 minutes. With a metal spatula, transfer to a rack to cool.

Cinnamon-Coated Cookies (top), Chewy Chocolate Biscuits

Chocolate Pretzels

MAKES 28

5 oz (140 g) plain flour
⅛ teaspoon salt
¾ oz (25 g) unsweetened cocoa powder
4 oz (115 g) butter, at room temperature
4½ oz (125 g) sugar
1 egg
1 egg white, lightly beaten, for glazing
sugar crystals, for sprinkling

1 Sift together the flour, salt and cocoa powder. Set aside. Grease 2 baking sheets.

2 ▲ With an electric mixer, cream the butter until light. Add the sugar and continue beating until light and fluffy. Beat in the egg. Add the dry ingredients and stir to blend. Gather the dough into a ball, wrap in clear film, and refrigerate for 1 hour or freeze for 30 minutes.

3 ▲ Roll the dough into 28 small balls. Refrigerate the balls until needed. Preheat the oven to 375°F/190°C/Gas 5.

4 ▲ Roll each ball into a rope about 10 in (25 cm) long. With each rope, form a loop with the two ends facing you. Twist the ends and fold back on to the circle, pressing in to make a pretzel shape. Place on the sheets.

5 ▲ Brush the pretzels with the egg white. Sprinkle sugar crystals over the tops and bake until firm, 10–12 minutes. Transfer to a rack to cool.

Cream Cheese Spirals

MAKES 32

8 oz (225 g) butter, at room temperature

8 oz (225 g) cream cheese

2 tsp caster sugar

8 oz (225 g) plain flour

1 egg white beaten with 1 tbsp water, for glazing

caster sugar, for sprinkling

FOR THE FILLING

4 oz (115 g) finely chopped walnuts

4 oz (115 g) light brown sugar

1 tsp ground cinnamon

1 With an electric mixer, cream the butter, cream cheese and sugar until soft. Sift over the flour and mix until combined. Gather into a ball and divide in half. Flatten each half, wrap in greaseproof paper and refrigerate for at least 30 minutes.

2 Meanwhile, make the filling. Mix together the chopped walnuts, the brown sugar and the cinnamon. Set aside.

3 Preheat a 375°F/190°F/Gas 5 oven. Grease 2 baking sheets.

4 ▲ Working with one half of the mixture at a time, roll out thinly into a circle about 11 in (28 cm) in diameter. Trim the edges with a knife, using a dinner plate as a guide.

5 ▼ Brush the surface with the egg white glaze and then sprinkle evenly with half the filling.

6 Cut the circle into quarters, and each quarter into 4 sections, to form 16 triangles.

7 ▲ Starting from the base of the triangles, roll up to form spirals.

8 Place on the sheets and brush with the remaining glaze. Sprinkle with caster sugar. Bake until golden, 15–20 minutes. Cool on a rack.

Vanilla Crescents

MAKES 36

6 oz (175 g) unblanched almonds

4 oz (115 g) plain flour

pinch of salt

8 oz (225 g) unsalted butter

4 oz (115 g) granulated sugar

1 teaspoon vanilla essence

icing sugar for dusting

1 Grind the almonds with a few tablespoons of the flour in a food processor, blender or nut grinder.

2 Sift the remaining flour with the salt into a bowl. Set aside.

3 With an electric mixer, cream together the butter and sugar until light and fluffy.

4 ▼ Add the almonds, vanilla essence and the flour mixture. Stir to mix well. Gather the dough into a ball, wrap in greaseproof paper, and chill for at least 30 minutes.

5 Preheat the oven to 325°F/170°C/ Gas 3. Lightly grease two baking sheets.

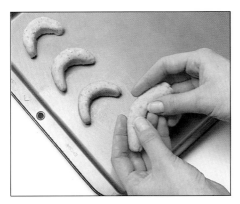

6 ▲ Break off walnut-size pieces of dough and roll into small cylinders about ½ in (1 cm) in diameter. Bend into small crescents and place on the prepared baking sheets.

7 Bake for about 20 minutes until dry but not brown. Transfer to a wire rack to cool only slightly. Set the rack over a baking sheet and dust with an even layer of icing sugar. Leave to cool completely.

Walnut Crescents

MAKES 72

4 oz (115 g) walnuts

8 oz (225 g) unsalted butter

4 oz (115 g) granulated sugar

½ teaspoon vanilla extract

8 oz (225 g) flour

¼ teaspoon salt

confectioners' sugar for dusting

1 Preheat the oven to 350°F/ 180°C/Gas 4.

2 Grind the walnuts in a food processor, blender or nut grinder until they are almost a paste. Transfer to a bowl.

3 Add the butter to the walnuts and mix with a wooden spoon until blended. Add the granulated sugar and vanilla and stir to blend.

4 ▼ Sift the flour and salt into the walnut mixture. Work into a dough.

5 Shape the dough into small cylinders about 1½ in (4 cm) long. Bend into crescents and place evenly spaced on an ungreased baking sheet.

6 ▲ Bake until lightly browned, about 15 minutes. Transfer to a rack to cool only slightly. Set the rack over a baking sheet and dust lightly with confectioners' sugar.

Vanilla Crescents (top), Walnut Crescents

Pecan Puffs

MAKES 24

4 oz (115 g) unsalted butter

2 tablespoons granulated sugar

pinch of salt

1 teaspoon vanilla essence

4 oz (115 g) pecans

4 oz (115 g) plain flour, sifted

icing sugar for dusting

1 Preheat the oven to 300°F/150°C/ Gas 2. Grease two baking sheets.

2 ▲ Cream the butter and sugar until light and fluffy. Stir in the salt and vanilla essence.

3 Grind the nuts in a food processor, blender or nut grinder. Stir several times to prevent nuts becoming oily. If necessary, grind in batches.

4 ▲ Push the ground nuts through a sieve set over a bowl to aerate them. Pieces too large to go through the sieve can be ground again.

5 ▲ Stir the nuts and flour into the butter mixture to make a firm, springy dough.

6 Roll the dough into marble-size balls between the palms of your hands. Place on the prepared baking sheets and bake for 45 minutes.

7 ▲ While the puffs are still hot, roll them in icing sugar. Leave to cool completely, then roll once more in icing sugar.

Pecan Tassies

Makes 24

4 oz (115 g) cream cheese
4 oz (115 g) butter
4 oz (115 g) plain flour
For the filling
2 eggs
4 oz (115 g) dark brown sugar
1 teaspoon vanilla essence
pinch of salt
2 tablespoons butter, melted
4 oz (115 g) pecans

1 Place a baking sheet in the oven and preheat to 350°F/180°C/Gas 4. Grease 24 mini-muffin tins.

2 Chop the cream cheese and butter into cubes. Put them in a mixing bowl. Sift over half the flour and mix. Add the remaining flour and continue mixing to form a dough.

3 ▲ Roll out the dough thinly. With a floured fluted pastry cutter, stamp out 24 2½ in/7cm rounds. Line the tins with the rounds and chill.

4 To make the filling, lightly whisk the eggs in a bowl. Gradually whisk in the brown sugar, and add the vanilla essence, salt and butter. Set aside until required.

5 ▼ Reserve 24 undamaged pecan halves and chop the rest coarsely with a sharp knife.

6 ▲ Place a spoonful of chopped nuts in each muffin tin and cover with the filling. Set a pecan half on the top of each.

7 Bake on the hot baking sheet for about 20 minutes, until puffed and set. Transfer to a wire rack to cool. Serve at room temperature.

~ VARIATION ~

To make Jam Tassies, fill the cream cheese pastry shells with raspberry or blackberry jam, or other fruit jams. Bake as described.

Lady Fingers

MAKES 18

3½ oz (90 g) plain flour

pinch of salt

4 eggs, separated

4 oz (115 g) granulated sugar

½ teaspoon vanilla essence

icing sugar for sprinkling

1 Preheat the oven to 300°F/150°C/ Gas 2. Grease 2 baking sheets, then coat lightly with flour, and shake off the excess.

2 Sift the flour and salt together twice in a bowl.

> ~ **COOK'S TIP** ~
>
> To make the biscuits all the same length, mark parallel lines 4 in (10 cm) apart on the greased baking sheets.

3 With an electric mixer beat the egg yolks with half of the sugar until thick enough to leave a ribbon trail when the beaters are lifted.

4 ▲ In another bowl, beat the egg whites until stiff. Beat in the remaining sugar until glossy.

5 Sift the flour over the yolks and spoon a large dollop of egg whites over the flour. Carefully fold in with a large metal spoon, adding the vanilla essence. Gently fold in the remaining whites.

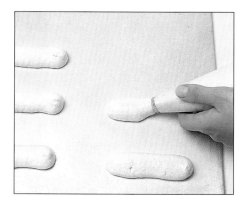

6 ▲ Spoon the mixture into a piping bag fitted with a large plain nozzle. Pipe 4 in (10 cm) long lines on the prepared baking sheets about 1 in (2.5 cm) apart. Sift over a layer of icing sugar. Turn the sheet upside down to dislodge any excess sugar.

7 Bake for about 20 minutes until crusty on the outside but soft in the centre. Cool slightly on the baking sheets before transferring to a wire rack to cool completely.

Walnut Cookies

MAKES 60

4 oz (115 g) butter or margarine

6 oz (175 g) caster sugar

4 oz (115 g) plain flour

2 teaspoons vanilla essence

4 oz (115 g) walnuts, finely chopped

> ~ **VARIATION** ~
>
> To make Almond Cookies, use an equal amount of finely chopped unblanched almonds instead of walnuts. Replace half the vanilla with ½ teaspoon almond essence.

1 Preheat the oven to 300°F/150°C/ Gas 2. Grease 2 baking sheets.

2 ▲ With an electric mixer, cream the butter or margarine until soft. Add 2 oz (50 g) of the sugar and continue beating until light and fluffy. Stir in the flour, vanilla essence and walnuts.

3 Drop teaspoonfuls of the batter 1–2 in (2.5–5 cm) apart on the prepared baking sheets and flatten slightly. Bake for about 25 minutes.

4 ▼ Transfer to a wire rack set over a baking sheet and sprinkle with the remaining sugar.

Lady Fingers (top), Walnut Cookies

Italian Almond Biscotti

MAKES 48

7 oz (200 g) whole unblanched almonds
7½ oz (215 g) plain flour
3½ oz (100 g) sugar
⅛ teaspoon salt
⅛ teaspoon saffron powder
½ teaspoon bicarbonate of soda
2 eggs
1 egg white, lightly beaten

~ COOK'S TIP ~

Serve biscotti after a meal, for dunking in glasses of sweet white wine, such as an Italian *Vin Santo* or a French *Muscat de Beaumes-de-Venise*.

1 Preheat a 375°F/190°C/Gas 5 oven. Grease and flour 2 baking sheets.

2 ▲ Spread the almonds in a baking tray and bake until lightly browned, about 15 minutes. When cool, grind 2 oz (55 g) of the almonds in a food processor, blender, or coffee grinder until pulverized. Coarsely chop the remaining almonds in 2 or 3 pieces each. Set aside.

3 ▲ Combine the flour, sugar, salt, saffron, bicarbonate of soda and ground almonds in a bowl and mix to blend. Make a well in the centre and add the eggs. Stir to form a rough dough. Transfer to a floured surface and knead until well blended. Knead in the chopped almonds.

4 ▲ Divide the dough into 3 equal parts. Roll into logs about 1 in (2.5 cm) in diameter. Place on one of the prepared sheets, brush with the egg white and bake for 20 minutes. Remove from the oven.

5 ▲ With a very sharp knife, cut into each log at an angle making ½ in (1 cm) slices. Return the slices on the baking sheets to a 275°F/140°C/Gas 1 oven and bake for 25 minutes more. Transfer to a rack to cool.

Christmas Cookies

MAKES 30

6 oz (170 g) unsalted butter, at room temperature

10 oz (285 g) caster sugar

1 egg

1 egg yolk

1 tsp vanilla essence

grated rind of 1 lemon

¼ tsp salt

10 oz (285 g) plain flour

FOR DECORATING (OPTIONAL)

coloured icing and small decorations

1 Preheat a 350°F/180°C/Gas 4 oven.

2 ▲ With an electric mixer, cream the butter until soft. Add the sugar gradually and continue beating until light and fluffy.

3 ▲ Using a wooden spoon, slowly mix in the whole egg and the egg yolk. Add the vanilla, lemon rind and salt. Stir to mix well.

4 Add the flour and stir until blended. Gather the mixture into a ball, wrap in greaseproof paper, and refrigerate for at least 30 minutes.

5 ▼ On a floured surface, roll out the mixture about ⅛ in (3 mm) thick.

6 ▲ Stamp out shapes or rounds with biscuit cutters.

7 Bake until lightly coloured, about 8 minutes. Transfer to a rack and let cool completely before icing and decorating, if wished.

Toasted Oat Meringues

MAKES 12

2 oz (55 g) rolled oats

2 egg whites

⅛ tsp salt

1½ tsp cornflour

6 oz (170 g) caster sugar

1 Preheat a 275°F/140°C/Gas 1 oven. Spread the oats on a baking sheet and toast in the oven until golden, about 10 minutes. Lower the heat to 250°F/130°C/Gas ½. Grease and flour a baking sheet.

~ **VARIATION** ~

Add ½ teaspoon ground cinnamon with the oats, and fold in gently.

2 ▼ With an electric mixer, beat the egg whites and salt until they start to form soft peaks.

3 Sift over the cornflour and continue beating until the whites hold stiff peaks. Add half the sugar and whisk until glossy.

4 ▲ Add the remaining sugar and fold in, then fold in the oats.

5 Gently spoon the mixture onto the prepared sheet and bake for 2 hours.

6 When done, turn off the oven. Lift the meringues from the sheet, turn over, and set in another place on the sheet to prevent sticking. Leave in the oven as it cools down.

Meringues

MAKES 24

4 egg whites

⅛ tsp salt

10 oz (285 g) caster sugar

½ tsp vanilla or almond essence (optional)

8 fl oz (250 ml) whipped cream (optional)

1 Preheat a 225°F/110°C/Gas ¼ oven. Grease and flour 2 large baking sheets.

2 With an electric mixer, beat the egg whites and salt in a very clean metal bowl on low speed. When they start to form soft peaks, add half the sugar and continue beating until the mixture holds stiff peaks.

3 ▲ With a large metal spoon, fold in the remaining sugar and vanilla or almond essence, if using.

4 ▼ Pipe the meringue mixture or gently spoon it on the prepared sheet.

5 Bake for 2 hours. Turn off the oven. Loosen the meringues, invert, and set in another place on the sheets to prevent sticking. Leave in the oven as it cools. Serve sandwiched with whipped cream, if wished.

Toasted Oat Meringues (top), Meringues

Chocolate Macaroons

MAKES 24

2 oz (55 g) plain chocolate
6 oz (170 g) blanched almonds
8 oz (225 g) caster sugar
3 egg whites
½ tsp vanilla essence
¼ tsp almond essence
icing sugar, for dusting

1 Preheat a 325°F/170°C/Gas 3 oven. Line 2 baking sheets with greaseproof paper and grease the paper.

2 ▼ Melt the chocolate in the top of a double boiler, or in a heatproof bowl set over a pan of hot water.

3 ▲ Grind the almonds finely in a food processor, blender or grinder. Transfer to a mixing bowl.

4 ▲ Add the sugar, egg whites, vanilla, and almond essence and stir to blend. Stir in the chocolate. The mixture should just hold its shape. If it is too soft, refrigerate for 15 minutes.

5 ▲ Use a teaspoon and your hands to shape the mixture into walnut-size balls. Place on the sheets and flatten slightly. Brush each ball with a little water and sift over a thin layer of icing sugar. Bake until just firm, 10–12 minutes. With a metal spatula, transfer to a rack to cool.

~ VARIATION ~

For Chocolate Pine Nut Macaroons, spread 3 oz (85 g) pine nuts in a shallow dish. Press the chocolate macaroon balls into the nuts to cover one side and bake as described, nut-side up.

Coconut Macaroons

MAKES 24

1½ oz (45 g) plain flour
⅛ tsp salt
8 oz (225 g) desiccated coconut
5½ fl oz (170 ml) sweetened condensed milk
1 tsp vanilla essence

1 Preheat a 350°F/180°C/Gas 4 oven. Grease 2 baking sheets.

2 Sift the flour and salt into a bowl. Stir in the coconut.

3 ▲ Pour in the milk. Add the vanilla and stir from the centre to make a very thick mixture.

4 ▼ Drop heaped tablespoonfuls of mixture 1 in (2.5 cm) apart on the sheets. Bake until golden brown, about 20 minutes. Cool on a rack.

Chocolate Macaroons (top), Coconut Macaroons

Almond Tiles

MAKES 40

2 oz (55 g) blanched almonds
4 oz (115 g) sugar
1¾ oz (50 g) unsalted butter
2 egg whites
1½ oz (45 g) plain flour
½ teaspoon vanilla essence
4 oz (115 g) slivered almonds

1 Grind the blanched almonds with 2 tablespoons of the sugar in a food processor, blender or nut grinder. If necessary, grind in batches.

2 Preheat the oven to 425°F/220°C/ Gas 7. Grease 2 baking sheets.

3 ▲ Put the butter in a large bowl and mix in the remaining sugar, using a metal spoon. With an electric mixer, cream them together until light and fluffy.

4 Add the egg whites and stir until blended. Sift over the flour and fold in with a metal spoon. Fold in the ground almonds and vanilla essence.

5 ▲ Working in small batches, drop tablespoonfuls of the mixture 3 in (7.5 cm) apart on one of the prepared sheets. With the back of a spoon, spread out into thin, almost transparent circles about 6 cm (2½ in) in diameter. Sprinkle each circle with some of the slivered almonds.

6 Bake until the outer edges have browned slightly, about 4 minutes.

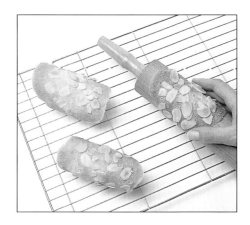

7 ▲ Remove from the oven. With a metal spatula, quickly drape the biscuits over a rolling pin to form a curved shape. Transfer to a rack when firm. If the biscuits harden too quickly to shape, reheat briefly. Repeat the baking and shaping process until the mixture is used up. Store in an airtight container.

Florentines

MAKES 36

1½ oz (45 g) butter
4 fl oz (125 ml) whipping cream
4½ oz (125 g) sugar
4½ oz (125 g) flaked almonds
2 oz (55 g) orange or mixed peel, finely chopped
1½ oz (45 g) glacé cherries, chopped
2½ oz (70 g) plain flour, sifted
8 oz (225 g) plain chocolate
1 teaspoon vegetable oil

1 Preheat the oven to 350°F/180°C/ Gas 4. Grease 2 baking sheets.

2 ▲ Melt the butter, cream and sugar together and slowly bring to the boil. Take off the heat and stir in the almonds, orange or mixed peel, cherries and flour until blended.

3 Drop teaspoonfuls of the batter 1–2 in (2.5–5 cm) apart on the prepared sheets and flatten with a fork.

4 Bake until the cookies brown at the edges, about 10 minutes. Remove from the oven and correct the shape by quickly pushing in any thin uneven edges with a knife or a round biscuit cutter. Work fast or they will cool and harden while still on the sheets. If necessary, return to the oven for a few moments to soften. While still hot, use a metal palette knife to transfer the florentines to a clean, flat surface.

5 Melt the chocolate in the top of a double boiler or in a heatproof bowl set over a pan of hot water. Add the oil and stir to blend.

6 ▲ With a metal palette knife, spread the smooth underside of the cooled florentines with a thin coating of the melted chocolate.

7 ▼ When the chocolate is about to set, draw a serrated knife across the surface with a slight sawing motion to make wavy lines. Store in an airtight container in a cool place.

Nut Lace Wafers

MAKES 18

2½ oz (70 g) whole blanched almonds

2 oz (55 g) butter

1½ oz (45 g) plain flour

3½ oz (100 g) sugar

1 fl oz (30 ml) double cream

½ teaspoon vanilla essence

1 Preheat the oven to 375°F/190°C/ Gas 5. Grease 1–2 baking sheets.

2 With a sharp knife, chop the almonds as fine as possible. Alternatively, use a food processor, blender, or coffee grinder to chop the nuts very fine.

3 ▼ Melt the butter in a saucepan over low heat. Remove from the heat and stir in the remaining ingredients and the almonds.

4 Drop teaspoonfuls 2½ in (6 cm) apart on the prepared sheets. Bake until golden, about 5 minutes. Cool on the baking sheets briefly, just until the wafers are stiff enough to remove.

5 ▲ With a metal palette knife, transfer to a rack to cool completely.

~ **VARIATION** ~

Add 2 oz (55 g) finely chopped orange peel to the mixture.

Oatmeal Lace Rounds

MAKES 36

5½ oz (150 g) butter or margarine

4½ oz (125 g) quick-cooking porridge oats

5¾ oz (165 g) dark brown sugar

5¼ oz (150 g) caster sugar

1½ oz (45 g) plain flour

¼ teaspoon salt

1 egg, lightly beaten

1 teaspoon vanilla essence

2½ oz (70 g) pecans or walnuts, finely chopped

1 Preheat the oven to 350°F/180°C/ Gas 4. Grease 2 baking sheets.

2 Melt the butter in a saucepan over low heat. Set aside.

3 In a mixing bowl, combine the oats, brown sugar, caster sugar, flour and salt.

4 ▲ Make a well in the centre and add the butter or margarine, egg and vanilla.

5 ▼ Mix until blended, then stir in the chopped nuts.

6 Drop rounded teaspoonfuls of the mixture about 2 in (5 cm) apart on the prepared sheets. Bake until lightly browned on the edges and bubbling, 5–8 minutes. Let cool on the sheet for 2 minutes, then transfer to a rack to cool completely.

Nut Lace Wafers (top), Oatmeal Lace Rounds

Raspberry Sandwich Biscuits

MAKES 32

6 oz (170 g) blanched almonds
6 oz (170 g) plain flour
6 oz (170 g) butter, at room temperature
4 oz (115 g) caster sugar
grated rind of 1 lemon
1 tsp vanilla essence
1 egg white
⅛ tsp salt
1 oz (30 g) flaked almonds
8 fl oz (250 ml) raspberry jam
1 tbsp fresh lemon juice

1 Place the blanched almonds and 3 tablespoons of the flour in a food processor, blender or grinder and process until finely ground. Set aside.

2 With an electric mixer, cream the butter and sugar together until light and fluffy. Stir in the lemon rind and vanilla. Add the ground almonds and remaining flour and mix well until combined. Gather into a ball, wrap in greaseproof paper, and refrigerate for at least 1 hour.

3 Preheat a 325°F/170°C/Gas 3 oven. Line 2 baking sheets with greaseproof paper.

4 Divide the biscuit mixture into 4 equal parts. Working with one section at a time, roll out to a thickness of ⅛ in (3 mm) on a lightly floured surface. With a 2½ in (6 cm) fluted pastry cutter, stamp out circles. Gather the scraps, roll out and stamp out more circles. Repeat with the remaining sections.

5 ▲ Using a ¾ in (2 cm) piping nozzle or pastry cutter, stamp out the centres from half the circles. Place the rings and circles 1 in (2.5 cm) apart on the prepared sheets.

6 ▲ Whisk the egg white with the salt until just frothy. Chop the flaked almonds. Brush only the biscuit rings with the egg white, then sprinkle over the almonds. Bake until very lightly browned, 12–15 minutes. Let cool for a few minutes on the sheets before transferring to a rack.

7 ▲ In a saucepan, melt the jam with the lemon juice until it comes to a simmer. Brush the jam over the biscuit circles and sandwich together with the rings. Store in an airtight container with sheets of greaseproof paper between the layers.

Brandysnaps

MAKES 18

2 oz (55 g) butter, at room temperature
5 oz (140 g) caster sugar
1 rounded tbsp golden syrup
1½ oz (45 g) plain flour
½ tsp ground ginger
FOR THE FILLING
8 fl oz (250 ml) whipping cream
2 tbsp brandy

1 With an electric mixer, cream together the butter and sugar until light and fluffy, then beat in the golden syrup. Sift over the flour and ginger and mix together.

2 ▲ Transfer the mixture to a work surface and knead until smooth. Cover and refrigerate for 30 minutes.

3 Preheat a 375°F/190°C/Gas 5 oven. Grease a baking sheet.

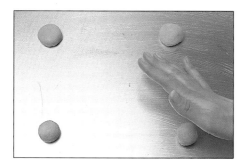

4 ▲ Working in batches of 4, form the mixture into walnut-size balls. Place far apart on the sheet and flatten slightly. Bake until golden and bubbling, about 10 minutes.

5 ▼ Remove from the oven and let cool a few moments. Working quickly, slide a metal spatula under each one, turn over, and wrap around the handle of a wooden spoon (have 4 spoons ready). If they firm up too quickly, reheat for a few seconds to soften. When firm, slide the snaps off and place on a rack to cool.

6 ▲ When all the brandy snaps are cool, prepare the filling. Whip the cream and brandy until soft peaks form. Fill a piping bag with the brandy cream. Pipe into each end of the brandy snaps just before serving.

Shortbread

MAKES 8

5½oz (150g) unsalted butter, at room temperature

3½oz (100g) caster sugar

6¼oz (180g) plain flour

2oz (55g) rice flour

¼ teaspoon baking powder

⅛ teaspoon salt

1 Preheat the oven to 325°F/170°C/Gas 3. Grease a shallow 8in(20cm) cake tin, preferably with a removable bottom.

2 With an electric mixer, cream the butter and sugar together until light and fluffy. Sift over the flours, baking powder and salt and mix well.

3 ▲ Press the dough neatly into the prepared tin, smoothing the surface with the back of a spoon.

4 Prick all over with a fork, then score into 8 equal wedges.

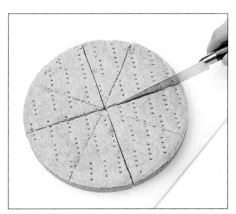

5 ▲ Bake until golden, 40–45 minutes. Leave in the tin until cool enough to handle, then turn out and recut the wedges while still hot. Store in an airtight container.

Flapjacks

MAKES 8

2oz (55g) butter

1 rounded tablespoon golden syrup

2¾oz (80g) dark brown sugar

3½oz (100g) quick-cooking porridge oats

⅛ teaspoon salt

1 ▲ Preheat a 350°F/180°C/Gas 4 oven. Line an 8in (20cm) cake tin with greaseproof paper and grease.

2 ▼ Place the butter, golden syrup and sugar in a saucepan over a low heat. Cook, stirring, until melted and combined.

~ VARIATION ~

If wished, add 1 teaspoon ground ginger to the melted butter.

3 ▲ Remove from the heat and add the oats and salt. Stir to blend.

4 Spoon into the prepared tin and smooth the surface. Place in the centre of the oven and bake until golden brown, 20–25 minutes. Leave in the tin until cool enough to handle, then turn out and cut into wedges while still hot.

Shortbread (top), Flapjacks

Chocolate Delights

MAKES 50

1 oz (30 g) plain chocolate
1 oz (30 g) bitter cooking chocolate
8 oz (225 g) plain flour
½ tsp salt
8 oz (225 g) unsalted butter, at room temperature
8 oz (225 g) caster sugar
2 eggs
1 tsp vanilla essence
4 oz (115 g) finely chopped walnuts

1 Melt the chocolates in the top of a double boiler, or in a heatproof bowl set over a pan of gently simmering water. Set aside.

2 ▼ In a small bowl, sift together the flour and salt. Set aside.

3 With an electric mixer, cream the butter until soft. Add the sugar and continue beating until the mixture is light and fluffy.

4 Mix the eggs and vanilla, then gradually stir into the butter mixture.

5 ▲ Stir in the chocolate, then the flour. Stir in the nuts.

6 ▲ Divide the mixture into 4 equal parts, and roll each into 2 in (5 cm) diameter logs. Wrap tightly in foil and refrigerate or freeze until firm.

7 Preheat a 375°F/190°C/Gas 5 oven. Grease 2 baking sheets.

8 With a sharp knife, cut the logs into ¼ in (5 mm) slices. Place the rounds on the prepared sheets and bake until lightly coloured, about 10 minutes. Transfer to a rack to cool.

~ **VARIATION** ~

For two-tone biscuits, melt only half the chocolate. Combine all the ingredients, except the chocolate, as above. Divide the mixture in half. Add the chocolate to one half. Roll out the plain mixture to a flat sheet. Roll out the chocolate mixture, place on top of the plain one and roll up. Wrap, slice and bake as described.

Cinnamon Treats

MAKES 50

9 oz (250 g) plain flour

½ tsp salt

2 tsp ground cinnamon

8 oz (225 g) unsalted butter, at room temperature

8 oz (225 g) caster sugar

2 eggs

1 tsp vanilla essence

1 In a bowl, sift together the flour, salt and cinnamon. Set aside.

2 ▲ With an electric mixer, cream the butter until soft. Add the sugar and continue beating until the mixture is light and fluffy.

3 Beat the eggs and vanilla, then gradually stir into the butter mixture.

4 ▲ Stir in the dry ingredients.

5 ▲ Divide the mixture into 4 equal parts, then roll each into 2 in (5 cm) diameter logs. Wrap tightly in foil and refrigerate or freeze until firm.

6 Preheat a 375°F/190°C/Gas 5 oven. Grease 2 baking sheets.

7 ▼ With a sharp knife, cut the logs into ¼ in (5 mm) slices. Place the rounds on the prepared sheets and bake until lightly coloured, about 10 minutes. With a metal spatula, transfer to a rack to cool.

Peanut Butter Biscuits

MAKES 24

5 oz (140 g) plain flour

½ teaspoon bicarbonate of soda

½ teaspoon salt

4 oz (115 g) butter, at room temperature

5¾ oz (165 g) light brown sugar

1 egg

1 teaspoon vanilla essence

9½ oz (265 g) crunchy peanut butter

1 Sift together the flour, bicarbonate of soda and salt and set aside.

2 With an electric mixer, cream the butter and sugar together until light and fluffy.

3 In another bowl, mix the egg and vanilla, then gradually beat into the butter mixture.

4 ▲ Stir in the peanut butter and blend thoroughly. Stir in the dry ingredients. Refrigerate for at least 30 minutes, or until firm.

5 Preheat the oven to 350°F/180°C/Gas 4. Grease 2 baking sheets.

6 Spoon out rounded teaspoonfuls of the dough and roll into balls.

7 ▲ Place the balls on the prepared sheets and press flat with a fork into circles about 2½ in (6 cm) in diameter, making a criss-cross pattern. Bake until lightly coloured, 12–15 minutes. Transfer to a rack to cool.

~ **VARIATION** ~

Add 3 oz (85 g) peanuts, coarsely chopped, with the peanut butter.

Chocolate Chip Cookies

MAKES 24

4 oz (115 g) butter or margarine, at room temperature

1¾ oz (50 g) caster sugar

3¾ oz (110 g) dark brown sugar

1 egg

½ teaspoon vanilla essence

6 oz (170 g) plain flour

½ teaspoon bicarbonate of soda

⅛ teaspoon salt

6 oz (170 g) chocolate chips

2 oz (55 g) walnuts, chopped

1 Preheat the oven to 350°F/180°C/Gas 4. Grease 2 large baking sheets.

2 ▼ With an electric mixer, cream the butter or margarine and two sugars together until light and fluffy.

3 In another bowl, mix the egg and vanilla, then gradually beat into the butter mixture. Sift over the flour, bicarbonate of soda and salt and stir.

4 ▲ Add the chocolate chips and walnuts, and mix to combine well.

5 Place heaped teaspoonfuls of the dough 2 in (5 cm) apart on the prepared sheets. Bake until lightly coloured, 10–15 minutes. Transfer to a rack to cool.

Peanut Butter Biscuits (top), Chocolate Chip Cookies

Salted Peanut Cookies

MAKES 70

12 oz (350 g) plain flour
½ teaspoon bicarbonate of soda
4 oz (115 g) butter
4 oz (115 g) margarine
9 oz (250 g) light brown sugar
2 eggs
2 teaspoons vanilla essence
8 oz (225 g) salted peanuts

1 Preheat the oven to 375°F/190°C/ Gas 5. Lightly grease 2 baking sheets. Grease the bottom of a glass and dip in sugar.

2 Sift together the flour and bicarbonate of soda. Set aside.

3 ▲ Cream the butter, margarine and sugar. Beat in the eggs and vanilla essence. Fold in the flour mixture.

4 ▲ Stir the peanuts into the butter mixture until evenly combined.

5 ▲ Drop teaspoonfuls 2 in (5 cm) apart on the prepared sheets. Flatten with the prepared glass.

6 Bake for about 10 minutes, until lightly coloured. With a metal spatula, transfer to a wire rack to cool.

~ **VARIATION** ~

To make Cashew Cookies, substitute an equal amount of salted cashews for the peanuts, and add as above.

Cheddar Pennies

MAKES 20

2 oz (50 g) butter
4 oz (115 g) Cheddar cheese, grated
1½ oz (40 g) plain flour
pinch of salt
pinch of chilli powder

1 Put the butter in a large bowl and cut into 1 in (2.5 cm) cubes. With an electric mixer, cream the butter until soft and fluffy.

2 ▲ Stir in the cheese, flour, salt and chilli. Gather to form a dough.

3 Transfer to a lightly floured surface. Shape into a cylinder about 1¼ in (3 cm) in diameter. Wrap in greaseproof paper and chill for 1–2 hours.

4 Preheat the oven to 350°F/180°C/ Gas 4. Grease 1–2 baking sheets.

5 ▲ Cut the dough into ¼ in (5 mm) thick slices and place on the prepared baking sheets. Bake for about 15 minutes, until golden. Transfer to a wire rack to cool.

Salted Peanut Cookies (top), Cheddar Pennies

Chocolate Chip Brownies

MAKES 24

4 oz (115 g) plain chocolate
4 oz (115 g) butter
3 eggs
7 oz (200 g) sugar
½ teaspoon vanilla essence
pinch of salt
5 oz (140 g) plain flour
6 oz (170 g) chocolate chips

1 ▼ Preheat a 350°F/180°C/Gas 4 oven. Line a 13 × 9 in (33 × 23 cm) tin with greaseproof paper and grease.

2 ▲ Melt the chocolate and butter in the top of a double boiler, or in a heatproof bowl set over a pan of gently simmering water.

3 ▲ Beat together the eggs, sugar, vanilla and salt. Stir in the chocolate mixture. Sift over the flour and fold in. Add the chocolate chips.

4 ▲ Pour the mixture into the prepared tin and spread evenly. Bake until just set, about 30 minutes. Do not overbake; the brownies should be slightly moist inside. Cool in the pan.

5 To turn out, run a knife all around the edge and invert onto a baking sheet. Remove the paper. Place another sheet on top and invert again so the brownies are right-side up. Cut into squares for serving.

Marbled Brownies

MAKES 24

8 oz (225 g) plain chocolate

3 oz (85 g) butter

4 eggs

10½ oz (300 g) sugar

5 oz (140 g) plain flour

½ teaspoon salt

1 teaspoon baking powder

2 teaspoons vanilla essence

4 oz (115 g) walnuts, chopped

FOR THE PLAIN MIXTURE

2 oz (55 g) butter, at room temperature

6 oz (170 g) cream cheese

3½ oz (100 g) sugar

2 eggs

1 oz (30 g) plain flour

1 teaspoon vanilla essence

1 Preheat a 350°F/180°C/Gas 4 oven. Line a 13 × 9 in (33 × 23 cm) tin with greaseproof paper and grease.

2 Melt the chocolate and butter over very low heat, stirring constantly. Set aside to cool.

3 Meanwhile, beat the eggs until light and fluffy. Gradually add the sugar and continue beating until blended. Sift over the flour, salt and baking powder and fold to combine.

4 ▲ Stir in the cooled chocolate mixture. Add the vanilla and walnuts. Measure and set aside 16 fl oz (450 ml) of the chocolate mixture.

5 ▲ For the plain mixture, cream the butter and cream cheese with an electric mixer.

6 Add the sugar and continue beating until blended. Beat in the eggs, flour and vanilla.

7 Spread the unmeasured chocolate mixture in the tin. Pour over the plain mixture. Drop spoonfuls of the reserved chocolate mixture on top.

8 ▲ With a metal palette knife, swirl the mixtures to marble. Do not blend completely. Bake until just set, 35–40 minutes. Turn out when cool and cut into squares for serving.

Nutty Chocolate Squares

MAKES 16

2 eggs

2 tsp vanilla essence

⅛ tsp salt

6 oz (170 g) pecan nuts, coarsely chopped

2 oz (55 g) plain flour

2 oz (55 g) caster sugar

4 fl oz (125 ml) golden syrup

3 oz (85 g) plain chocolate, finely chopped

1½ oz (45 g) butter

16 pecan halves, for decorating

1 Preheat a 325°F/170°C/Gas 3 oven. Line the bottom and sides of an 8 in (20 cm) square baking tin with greaseproof paper and grease lightly.

2 ▼ Whisk together the eggs, vanilla and salt. In another bowl, mix together the pecans and flour. Set both aside.

3 In a saucepan, bring the sugar and golden syrup to a boil. Remove from the heat and stir in the chocolate and butter and blend thoroughly with a wooden spoon.

4 ▲ Mix in the beaten eggs, then fold in the pecan mixture.

5 Pour the mixture into the prepared tin and bake until set, about 35 minutes. Cool in the tin for 10 minutes before unmoulding. Cut into 2 in (5 cm) squares and press pecan halves into the tops while warm. Cool completely on a rack.

Raisin Brownies

MAKES 16

4 oz (115 g) butter or margarine

2 oz (55 g) cocoa powder

2 eggs

8 oz (225 g) caster sugar

1 tsp vanilla essence

1½ oz (45 g) plain flour

3 oz (85 g) chopped walnuts

3 oz (85 g) raisins

1 Preheat a 350°F/180°C/Gas 4 oven. Line the bottom and sides of an 8 in (20 cm) square baking tin with greaseproof paper and grease the paper.

2 ▼ Gently melt the butter or margarine in a small saucepan. Remove from the heat and stir in the cocoa powder.

3 With an electric mixer, beat the eggs, sugar and vanilla together until light. Add the cocoa mixture and stir to blend.

4 ▲ Sift the flour over the cocoa mixture and gently fold in. Add the walnuts and raisins and scrape the mixture into the prepared tin.

5 Bake in the centre of the oven for 30 minutes. Do not overbake. Leave in the tin to cool before cutting into 2 in (5 cm) squares and removing. The brownies should be soft and moist.

Nutty Chocolate Squares (top), Raisin Brownies

Chocolate Walnut Bars

MAKES 24

2 oz (55 g) walnuts
2¼ oz (60 g) caster sugar
3¾ oz (110 g) plain flour, sifted
3 oz (85 g) cold unsalted butter, cut into pieces
FOR THE TOPPING
1 oz (30 g) unsalted butter
3 fl oz (85 ml) water
1 oz (30 g) unsweetened cocoa powder
3½ oz (100 g) caster sugar
1 teaspoon vanilla essence
⅛ teaspoon salt
2 eggs
icing sugar, for dusting

1 Preheat a 350°F/180°C/Gas 4 oven. Grease the bottom and sides of an 8 in (20 cm) square baking tin.

2 ▼ Grind the walnuts with a few tablespoons of the sugar in a food processor, blender or coffee grinder.

3 In a bowl, combine the ground walnuts, remaining sugar and flour. With your fingertips, rub in the butter until the mixture resembles coarse breadcrumbs. Alternatively, process all the ingredients in a food processor until the mixture resembles coarse breadcrumbs.

4 ▲ Pat the walnut mixture into the bottom of the prepared tin in an even layer. Bake for 25 minutes.

5 ▲ Meanwhile, for the topping, melt the butter with the water. Whisk in the cocoa and sugar. Remove from the heat, stir in the vanilla and salt and let cool for 5 minutes. Whisk in the eggs until blended.

6 ▲ Pour the topping over the crust when baked.

7 Return to the oven and bake until set, about 20 minutes. Set the tin on a rack to cool. Cut into 2½ × 1 in (6 × 2.5 cm) bars and dust with icing sugar. Store in the refrigerator.

Pecan Squares

MAKES 36

8 oz (225 g) plain flour
pinch of salt
4 oz (115 g) granulated sugar
8 oz (225 g) cold butter or margarine, chopped
1 egg
finely grated rind of 1 lemon
FOR THE TOPPING
6 oz (175 g) butter
3 oz (75 g) honey
2 oz (50 g) granulated sugar
4 oz (115 g) dark brown sugar
5 tablespoons whipping cream
1 lb (450 g) pecan halves

1 Preheat the oven to 375°F/190°C/ Gas 5. Lightly grease a 15½ × 10½ × 1 in (37 × 27 × 2.5 cm) Swiss roll tin.

2 ▲ Sift the flour and salt into a mixing bowl. Stir in the sugar. Cut and rub in the butter or margarine until the mixture resembles coarse crumbs. Add the egg and lemon rind and blend with a fork until the mixture just holds together.

3 ▼ Spoon the mixture into the prepared tin. With floured fingertips, press into an even layer. Prick the pastry all over with a fork and chill for 10 minutes.

4 Bake the pastry crust for 15 minutes. Remove the tin from the oven, but keep the oven on while making the topping.

5 ▲ To make the topping, melt the butter, honey and both sugars. Bring to the boil. Boil, without stirring, for 2 minutes. Off the heat, stir in the cream and pecans. Pour over the crust, return to the oven and bake for 25 minutes. Leave to cool.

6 When cool, run a knife around the edge. Invert on to a baking sheet, place another sheet on top and invert again. Dip a sharp knife into very hot water and cut into squares for serving.

Figgy Bars

MAKES 48

12 oz (350 g) dried figs
3 eggs
6 oz (170 g) caster sugar
3 oz (85 g) plain flour
1 tsp baking powder
½ tsp ground cinnamon
¼ tsp ground cloves
¼ tsp grated nutmeg
¼ tsp salt
3 oz (85 g) finely chopped walnuts
2 tbsp brandy or cognac
icing sugar, for dusting

1 Preheat a 325°F/170°C/Gas 3 oven.

2 Line a 12 × 8 × 1½ in (30 × 20 × 3 cm) tin with greaseproof paper and grease the paper.

3 ▲ With a sharp knife, chop the figs roughly. Set aside.

4 In a bowl, whisk the eggs and sugar until well blended. In another bowl, sift together the dry ingredients, then fold into the egg mixture in several batches.

5 ▼ Stir in the figs, walnuts and brandy or cognac.

6 Scrape the mixture into the prepared tin and bake until the top is firm and brown, 35–40 minutes. It should still be soft underneath.

7 Let cool in the tin for 5 minutes, then unmould and transfer to a sheet of greaseproof paper lightly sprinkled with icing sugar. Cut into bars.

Lemon Bars

MAKES 36

2 oz (55 g) icing sugar
6 oz (170 g) plain flour
½ tsp salt
6 oz (170 g) butter, cut in small pieces
FOR THE TOPPING
4 eggs
12 oz (350 g) caster sugar
grated rind of 1 lemon
4 fl oz (125 ml) fresh lemon juice
6 fl oz (175 ml) whipping cream
icing sugar, for dusting

1 Preheat a 325°F/170°C/Gas 3 oven.

2 Grease a 13 × 9 in (33 × 23 cm) baking tin.

3 Sift the sugar, flour and salt into a bowl. With a pastry blender, cut in the butter until the mixture resembles coarse breadcrumbs.

4 ▲ Press the mixture into the bottom of the prepared tin. Bake until golden brown, about 20 minutes.

5 Meanwhile, for the topping, whisk the eggs and sugar together until blended. Add the lemon rind and juice and mix well.

6 ▲ Lightly whip the cream and fold into the egg mixture. Pour over the still warm base, return to the oven, and bake until set, about 40 minutes.

7 Cool completely before cutting into bars. Dust with icing sugar.

Figgy Bars (top), Lemon Bars

Apricot Specials

MAKES 12

3½ oz (100 g) light brown sugar
3 oz (85 g) plain flour
3 oz (85 g) cold unsalted butter, cut in pieces
FOR THE TOPPING
5 oz (140 g) dried apricots
8 fl oz (250 ml) water
grated rind of 1 lemon
2½ oz (75 g) caster sugar
2 tsp cornflour
2 oz (55 g) chopped walnuts

1 Preheat a 350°F/180°C/Gas 4 oven.

2 ▲ In a bowl, combine the brown sugar and flour. With a pastry blender, cut in the butter until the mixture resembles coarse breadcrumbs.

3 ▲ Transfer to an 8 in (20 cm) square baking tin and press level. Bake for 15 minutes. Remove from the oven but leave the oven on.

4 Meanwhile, for the topping, combine the apricots and water in a saucepan and simmer until soft, about 10 minutes. Strain the liquid and reserve. Chop the apricots.

5 ▲ Return the apricots to the saucepan and add the lemon rind, caster sugar, cornflour, and 4 tablespoons of the soaking liquid. Cook for 1 minute.

6 ▲ Cool slightly before spreading the topping over the base. Sprinkle over the walnuts and continue baking for 20 minutes more. Let cool in the tin before cutting into bars.

Almond-Topped Squares

MAKES 18

3 oz (75 g) butter

2 oz (50 g) granulated sugar

1 egg yolk

grated rind and juice of ½ lemon

½ teaspoon vanilla essence

2 tablespoons whipping cream

4 oz (115 g) plain flour

FOR THE TOPPING

8 oz (225 g) granulated sugar

3 oz (75 g) sliced almonds

4 egg whites

½ teaspoon ground ginger

½ teaspoon ground cinnamon

4 With lightly floured fingers, press the dough into the prepared tin. Bake for 15 minutes. Remove from the oven but leave the oven on.

5 ▲ To make the topping, combine all the ingredients in a heavy saucepan. Cook, stirring until the mixture comes to the boil.

6 Continue boiling until just golden, about 1 minute. Pour over the dough, spreading evenly.

7 ▲ Return to the oven and bake for about 45 minutes. Remove and score into bars or squares. Cool completely before cutting into squares and serving.

1 ▲ Preheat the oven to 375°F/ 190°C/Gas 5. Line a 13 x 9 in (33 x 23 cm) Swiss roll tin with greaseproof paper and grease the paper.

2 Cream the butter and sugar. Beat in the egg yolk, lemon rind and juice, vanilla essence and cream.

3 ▲ Gradually stir in the flour. Gather into a ball of dough.

Spiced Raisin Bars

MAKES 30

3¾ oz (110 g) plain flour

1½ teaspoons baking powder

1 teaspoon ground cinnamon

½ teaspoon grated nutmeg

¼ teaspoon ground cloves

¼ teaspoon ground allspsice

7½ oz (215 g) raisins

4 oz (115 g) butter or margarine, at room temperature

3½ oz (100 g) sugar

2 eggs

5¾ oz (165 g) molasses

2 oz (55 g) walnuts, chopped

1 Preheat a 350°F/180°C/Gas 4 oven. Line a 13 × 9 in (33 × 23 cm) tin with greaseproof paper and grease.

2 Sift together the flour, baking powder and spices.

3 ▲ Place the raisins in another bowl and toss with a few tablespoons of the flour mixture.

4 ▲ With an electric mixer, cream the butter or margarine and sugar together until light and fluffy. Beat in the eggs, 1 at a time, then the molasses. Stir in the flour mixture, raisins and walnuts.

5 Spread evenly in the tin. Bake until just set, 15–18 minutes. Let cool in the tin before cutting into bars.

Toffee Meringue Bars

MAKES 12

2 oz (55 g) butter

7½ oz (215 g) dark brown sugar

1 egg

½ teaspoon vanilla essence

2½ oz (70 g) plain flour

½ teaspoon salt

¼ teaspoon grated nutmeg

FOR THE TOPPING

1 egg white

⅛ teaspoon salt

1 tablespoon golden syrup

3½ oz (100 g) caster sugar

2 oz (55 g) walnuts, finely chopped

1 ▲ Combine the butter and brown sugar in a saucepan and heat until bubbling. Set aside to cool.

2 Preheat the oven to 350°F/180°C/ Gas 4. Line the bottom and sides of an 8 in (20 cm) square cake tin with greaseproof paper and grease.

3 Beat the egg and vanilla into cooled sugar mixture. Sift over the flour, salt and nutmeg and fold in. Spread in the bottom of the tin.

4 ▲ For the topping, beat the egg white with the salt until it holds soft peaks. Beat in the golden syrup, then the sugar and continue beating until the mixture holds stiff peaks. Fold in the nuts and spread on top. Bake for 30 minutes. Cut into bars when cool.

Spiced Raisin Bars (top), Toffee Meringue Bars

BUNS & TEA BREADS

~

*Easy to make and satisfying to eat, these buns and tea breads
will fill the house with mouthwatering scents and lure your
family and friends to linger over breakfast, coffee or tea –
and they are great for snacks or lunch.*

Blueberry Muffins

MAKES 12

6¼ oz (180 g) plain flour
2¼ oz (60 g) sugar
2 teaspoons baking powder
¼ teaspoon salt
2 eggs
2 oz (55 g) butter, melted
6 fl oz (175 ml) milk
1 teaspoon vanilla essence
1 teaspoon grated lemon rind
6 oz (170 g) fresh blueberries

1 Preheat a 400°F/200°C/Gas 6 oven.

2 ▼ Grease a 12-cup muffin tin or use paper cases.

3 ▲ Sift the flour, sugar, baking powder and salt into a bowl.

4 In another bowl, whisk the eggs until blended. Add the melted butter, milk, vanilla and lemon rind and stir to combine.

5 Make a well in the dry ingredients and pour in the egg mixture. With a large metal spoon, stir just until the flour is moistened, not until smooth.

6 ▲ Fold in the blueberries.

7 ▲ Spoon the batter into the cups, leaving room for the muffins to rise.

8 Bake until the tops spring back when touched lightly, 20–25 minutes. Let cool in the pan for 5 minutes before turning out.

Apple and Cranberry Muffins

MAKES 12

2 oz (55 g) butter or margarine
1 egg
3½ oz (100 g) sugar
grated rind of 1 large orange
4 fl oz (125 ml) freshly squeezed orange juice
5 oz (140 g) plain flour
1 teaspoon baking powder
½ teaspoon bicarbonate of soda
1 teaspoon ground cinnamon
½ teaspoon grated nutmeg
½ teaspoon ground allspice
¼ teaspoon ground ginger
¼ teaspoon salt
1–2 dessert apples
6 oz (170 g) cranberries
2 oz (55 g) walnuts, chopped
icing sugar, for dusting (optional)

1 Preheat the oven to 350°F/180°C/ Gas 4. Grease a 12-cup muffin tin or use paper cases.

2 Melt the butter or margarine over gentle heat. Set aside to cool.

3 ▲ Place the egg in a mixing bowl and whisk lightly. Add the melted butter or margarine and whisk to combine.

4 Add the sugar, orange rind and juice. Whisk to blend, then set aside.

5 In a large bowl, sift together the flour, baking powder, bicarbonate of soda, cinnamon, nutmeg, allspice, ginger and salt. Set aside.

6 ▲ Quarter, core and peel the apples. With a sharp knife, chop coarsely.

7 Make a well in the dry ingredients and pour in the egg mixture. With a spoon, stir until just blended.

8 ▲ Add the apples, cranberries and walnuts and stir to blend.

9 Fill the cups three-quarters full and bake until the tops spring back when touched lightly, 25–30 minutes. Transfer to a rack to cool. Dust with icing sugar, if desired.

Chocolate Chip Muffins

MAKES 10

4 oz (115 g) butter or margarine, at room temperature

2½ oz (70 g) caster sugar

1 oz (30 g) dark brown sugar

2 eggs, at room temperature

7½ oz (215 g) plain flour

1 teaspoon baking powder

4 fl oz (125 ml) milk

6 oz (170 g) plain chocolate chips

1 Preheat the oven to 375°F/190°C/ Gas 5. Grease 10 muffin cups or use paper cases.

2 ▼ With an electric mixer, cream the butter until soft. Add both sugars and beat until light and fluffy. Beat in the eggs, 1 at a time.

3 Sift together the flour and baking powder, twice. Fold into the butter mixture, alternating with the milk.

4 ▲ Divide half the mixture between the muffin cups. Sprinkle several chocolate chips on top, then cover with a spoonful of the batter. To ensure even baking, half-fill any empty cups with water.

5 Bake until lightly coloured, about 25 minutes. Let stand 5 minutes before turning out.

Chocolate Walnut Muffins

MAKES 12

6 oz (170 g) unsalted butter

5 oz (140 g) plain chocolate

7 oz (200 g) caster sugar

2 oz (55 g) dark brown sugar

4 eggs

1 teaspoon vanilla essence

¼ teaspoon almond essence

3¾ oz (110 g) plain flour

1 tablespoon unsweetened cocoa powder

4 oz (115 g) walnuts, chopped

1 Preheat the oven to 350°F/180°C/ Gas 4. Grease a 12-cup muffin pan or use paper cases.

2 ▼ Melt the butter with the chocolate in the top of a double boiler or in a heatproof bowl set over a pan of hot water. Transfer to a large mixing bowl.

3 Stir both the sugars into the chocolate mixture. Mix in the eggs, 1 at a time, then add the vanilla and almond essences.

4 Sift over the flour and cocoa.

5 ▲ Fold in and stir in the walnuts.

6 Fill the prepared cups almost to the top and bake until a skewer inserted in the centre barely comes out clean, 30–35 minutes. Let stand 5 minutes before turning out onto a rack to cool completely.

Chocolate Chip Muffins (top), Chocolate Walnut Muffins

Raisin Bran Buns

MAKES 15

2 oz (55 g) butter or margarine

1½ oz (45 g) plain flour

2 oz (55 g) wholewheat flour

1½ tsp bicarbonate of soda

⅛ tsp salt

1 tsp ground cinnamon

1 oz (30 g) bran

3 oz (85 g) raisins

2½ oz (65 g) dark brown sugar

2 oz (55 g) caster sugar

1 egg

8 fl oz (250 ml) buttermilk

juice of ½ lemon

1 Preheat a 400°F/200°C/Gas 6 oven. Grease 15 bun-tray cups.

2 ▲ Place the butter or margarine in a saucepan and melt over gentle heat. Set aside.

3 In a mixing bowl, sift together the flours, bicarbonate of soda, salt and cinnamon.

4 ▲ Add the bran, raisins and sugars and stir until blended.

5 In another bowl, mix together the egg, buttermilk, lemon juice and melted butter.

6 ▲ Add the buttermilk mixture to the dry ingredients and stir lightly and quickly just until moistened; do not mix until smooth.

7 ▲ Spoon the mixture into the prepared bun tray, filling the cups almost to the top. Half-fill any empty cups with water.

8 Bake until golden, 15–20 minutes. Serve warm or at room temperature.

Raspberry Crumble Buns

MAKES 12

6 oz (170 g) plain flour
2 oz (55 g) caster sugar
1¾ oz (50 g) light brown sugar
2 tsp baking powder
⅛ tsp salt
1 tsp ground cinnamon
4 oz (115 g) butter, melted
1 egg
4 fl oz (125 ml) milk
5 oz (140 g) fresh raspberries
grated rind of 1 lemon
FOR THE CRUMBLE TOPPING
1 oz (30 g) finely chopped pecan nuts or walnuts
2 oz (55 g) dark brown sugar
3 tbsp plain flour
1 tsp ground cinnamon
3 tbsp butter, melted

1 Preheat a 350°F/180°C/Gas 4 oven. Grease a 12-cup bun tray or use paper cases.

2 Sift the flour into a bowl. Add the sugars, baking powder, salt and cinnamon and stir to blend.

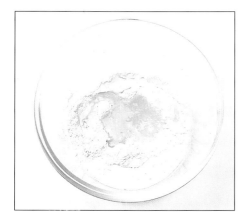

3 ▲ Make a well in the centre. Place the butter, egg and milk in the well and mix until just combined. Stir in the raspberries and lemon rind. Spoon the mixture into the prepared bun tray, filling the cups almost to the top.

4 ▼ For the crumble topping, mix the nuts, dark brown sugar, flour and cinnamon in a bowl. Add the melted butter and stir to blend.

5 ▲ Spoon some of the crumble over each bun. Bake until browned, about 25 minutes. Transfer to a rack to cool slightly. Serve warm.

Carrot Buns

MAKES 12

6 oz (170 g) margarine, at room temperature

3½ oz (100 g) dark brown sugar

1 egg, at room temperature

1 tbsp water

8 oz (225 g) carrots, grated

5 oz (140 g) plain flour

1 tsp baking powder

½ tsp bicarbonate of soda

1 tsp ground cinnamon

¼ tsp grated nutmeg

½ tsp salt

1 Preheat a 350°F/180°C/Gas 4 oven. Grease a 12-cup bun tray or use paper cases.

2 With an electric mixer, cream the margarine and sugar until light and fluffy. Beat in the egg and water.

3 ▲ Stir in the carrots.

4 Sift over the flour, baking powder, bicarbonate of soda, cinnamon, nutmeg and salt. Stir to blend.

5 ▼ Spoon the mixture into the prepared bun tray, filling the cups almost to the top. Bake until the tops spring back when touched lightly, about 35 minutes. Let stand 10 minutes before transferring to a rack.

Dried Cherry Buns

MAKES 16

8 fl oz (250 ml) plain yoghurt

6 oz (170 g) dried cherries

4 oz (115 g) butter, at room temperature

6 oz (170 g) caster sugar

2 eggs, at room temperature

1 tsp vanilla essence

7 oz (200 g) plain flour

2 tsp baking powder

1 tsp bicarbonate of soda

⅛ tsp salt

1 In a mixing bowl, combine the yoghurt and cherries. Cover and let stand for 30 minutes.

2 Preheat a 350°F/180°C/Gas 4 oven. Grease 16 bun-tray cups or use paper cases.

3 With an electric mixer, cream the butter and sugar together until light and fluffy.

4 ▼ Add the eggs, 1 at a time, beating well after each addition. Add the vanilla and the cherry mixture and stir to blend. Set aside.

5 ▲ In another bowl, sift together the flour, baking powder, bicarbonate soda and salt. Fold into the cherry mixture in 3 batches.

6 Fill the prepared cups two-thirds full. For even baking, half-fill any empty cups with water. Bake until the tops spring back when touched lightly, about 20 minutes. Transfer to a rack to cool.

Carrot Buns (top), Dried Cherry Buns

Oat and Raisin Muffins

MAKES 12

3 oz (85 g) rolled oats
8 fl oz (250 ml) buttermilk
4 oz (120 g) butter, at room temperature
3½ oz (100 g) dark brown sugar
1 egg, at room temperature
4 oz (120 g) flour
1 teaspoon baking powder
½ teaspoon bicarbonate of soda
¼ teaspoon salt
1 oz (30 g) raisins

~ COOK'S TIP ~

If buttermilk is not available, add
1 teaspoon lemon juice or vinegar
to milk. Let the mixture stand
for a few minutes to curdle.

1 ▲ In a bowl, combine the oats and buttermilk and let soak for 1 hour.

2 ▲ Lightly grease a 12-cup muffin tin or use paper cases.

3 ▲ Preheat the oven to 400°F/ 200°C/Gas 6. With an electric mixer, cream the butter and sugar until light and fluffy. Beat in the egg.

4 In another bowl, sift the flour, baking powder, bicarbonate of soda and salt. Stir into the butter mixture, alternating with the oat mixture. Fold in the raisins. Do not overmix.

5 Fill the prepared cups two-thirds full. Bake until a skewer inserted in the centre comes out clean, 20–25 minutes. Transfer to a rack to cool.

Pumpkin Muffins

MAKES 14

4 oz (120 g) butter or margarine, at room temperature
5 oz (150 g) dark brown sugar
4 tablespoons molasses
1 egg, at room temperature, beaten
8 oz (225 g) cooked or canned pumpkin
8 oz (225 g) flour
¼ teaspoon salt
1 teaspoon bicarbonate of soda
1½ teaspoons ground cinnamon
1 teaspoon grated nutmeg
1 oz (30 g) currants or raisins

1 Preheat the oven to 400°F/200°C/ Gas 6. Grease 14 muffin cups or use paper cases.

2 With an electric mixer, cream the butter or margarine until soft. Add the sugar and molasses and beat until light and fluffy.

3 ▲ Add the egg and pumpkin and stir until well blended.

4 Sift over the flour, salt, bicarbonate of soda, cinnamon and nutmeg. Fold just enough to blend; do not overmix.

5 ▼ Fold in the currants or raisins.

6 Spoon the mixture into the prepared muffin cups, filling them three-quarters full.

7 Bake until the tops spring back when touched lightly, 12–15 minutes. Serve warm or cold.

Prune Muffins

MAKES 12

1 egg

8 fl oz (250 ml) milk

4 fl oz (125 ml) vegetable oil

1¾ oz (50 g) caster sugar

1 oz (30 g) dark brown sugar

10 oz (285 g) plain flour

2 teaspoons baking powder

½ teaspoon salt

¼ teaspoon grated nutmeg

4 oz (115 g) cooked stoned prunes, chopped

1 Preheat a 400°F/200°C/Gas 6 oven. Grease a 12-cup muffin tin.

2 Break the egg into a mixing bowl and beat with a fork. Beat in the milk and oil.

3 ▼ Stir in the sugars. Set aside.

4 Sift the flour, baking powder, salt and nutmeg into a mixing bowl. Make a well in the centre, pour in the egg mixture and stir until moistened. Do not overmix; the batter should be slightly lumpy.

5 ▲ Fold in the prunes.

6 Fill the prepared cups two-thirds full. Bake until golden brown, about 20 minutes. Let stand 10 minutes before turning out. Serve warm or at room temperature.

Yogurt and Honey Muffins

MAKES 12

2 oz (55 g) butter

5 tablespoons clear honey

8 fl oz (250 ml) plain yogurt

1 large egg, at room temperature

grated rind of 1 lemon

2 fl oz (65 ml) lemon juice

5 oz (140 g) plain flour

6 oz (170 g) wholemeal flour

1½ teaspoons bicarbonate of soda

⅛ teaspoon grated nutmeg

~ **VARIATION** ~

For Walnut Yogurt Honey Muffins, add 2 oz (55 g) chopped walnuts, folded in with the flour. This makes a more substantial muffin.

1 Preheat a 375°F/190°C/Gas 5 oven. Grease a 12-cup muffin tin or use paper cases.

2 In a saucepan, melt the butter and honey. Remove from the heat and set aside to cool slightly.

3 ▲ In a bowl, whisk together the yogurt, egg, lemon rind and juice. Add the butter and honey mixture. Set aside.

4 ▲ In another bowl, sift together the dry ingredients.

5 Fold the dry ingredients into the yogurt mixture to blend.

6 Fill the prepared cups two-thirds full. Bake until the tops spring back when touched lightly, 20–25 minutes. Let cool in the tin for 5 minutes before turning out. Serve warm or at room temperature.

Prune Muffins (top), Yogurt and Honey Muffins

Banana Muffins

MAKES 10

9 oz (250 g) plain flour

1 teaspoon baking powder

1 teaspoon bicarbonate of soda

¼ teaspoon salt

½ teaspoon ground cinnamon

¼ teaspoon grated nutmeg

3 large ripe bananas

1 egg

2½ oz (70 g) dark brown sugar

2 fl oz (50 ml) vegetable oil

1 oz (30 g) raisins

1 ▼ Preheat the oven to 375°F/190°C/Gas 5. Lightly grease or line 10 deep muffin tins with paper cases.

2 Sift together the flour, baking powder, bicarbonate of soda, salt, cinnamon and nutmeg. Set aside.

3 ▲ With an electric mixer, beat the peeled bananas at moderate speed until mashed.

4 ▲ Beat in the egg, sugar and oil.

5 Add the dry ingredients and beat in gradually, on low speed. Mix just until blended. With a wooden spoon, stir in the raisins.

6 Fill the prepared cups two-thirds full. For even baking, half-fill any empty cups with water.

7 ▲ Bake until the tops spring back when touched lightly, 20–25 minutes. Transfer to a rack to cool.

Maple Pecan Muffins

MAKES 20

6 oz (170 g) pecans

12 oz (340 g) flour

1 teaspoon baking powder

1 teaspoon bicarbonate of soda

¼ teaspoon salt

¼ teaspoon ground cinnamon

3½ oz (100 g) caster sugar

2½ oz (70 g) light brown sugar

3 tablespoons maple syrup

5 oz (150 g) butter, at room temperature

3 eggs, at room temperature

½ pint (300 ml) buttermilk

60 pecan halves, for decorating

1 Preheat the oven to 350°F/180°C/ Gas 4. Lightly grease 24 deep muffin tins or use paper cases.

2 ▲ Spread the pecans on a baking sheet and toast in the oven for 5 minutes. When cool, chop coarsely and set aside.

~ **VARIATION** ~

For Pecan Spice Muffins, substitute an equal quantity of golden syrup for the maple syrup. Increase the cinnamon to ½ teaspoon, and add 1 teaspoon ground ginger and ½ teaspoon grated nutmeg, sifted with the dry ingredients.

3 In a bowl, sift together the flour, baking powder, bicarbonate of soda, salt and cinnamon. Set aside.

4 ▲ In a large mixing bowl, combine the caster sugar, light brown sugar, maple syrup and butter. Beat with an electric mixer until light and fluffy.

5 Add the eggs, 1 at a time, beating to incorporate thoroughly after each addition.

6 ▲ Pour half the buttermilk and half the dry ingredients into the butter mixture, then stir until blended. Repeat with the remaining buttermilk and dry ingredients.

7 Fold in the chopped pecans. Fill the prepared cups two-thirds full. Top with the pecan halves. For even baking, half-fill any empty cups with water.

8 Bake until puffed up and golden, 20–25 minutes. Let stand 5 minutes before unmoulding.

Cheese Muffins

MAKES 9

2 oz (55 g) butter

7 oz (200 g) plain flour

2 teaspoons baking powder

2 tablespoons sugar

¼ teaspoon salt

1 teaspoon paprika

2 eggs

4 fl oz (125 ml) milk

1 teaspoon dried thyme

2 oz (55 g) mature Cheddar cheese, cut into ½ in (1 cm) dice

1 Preheat the oven to 375°F/190°C/ Gas 5. Thickly grease 9 deep muffin tins or use paper cases.

2 Melt the butter and set aside.

3 ▼ In a mixing bowl, sift together the flour, baking powder, sugar, salt and paprika.

4 ▲ In another bowl, combine the eggs, milk, melted butter and thyme, and whisk to blend.

5 Add the milk mixture to the dry ingredients and stir just until moistened; do not mix until smooth.

6 ▲ Place a heaped spoonful of batter into the prepared cups. Drop a few pieces of cheese over each, then top with another spoonful of batter. For even baking, half-fill any empty muffin cups with water.

7 ▲ Bake until puffed and golden, about 25 minutes. Let stand 5 minutes before unmoulding on to a rack. Serve warm or at room temperature.

Bacon and Cornmeal Muffins

MAKES 14

8 bacon rashers

2 oz (55 g) butter

2 oz (55 g) margarine

4 oz (120 g) plain flour

1 tablespoon baking powder

1 teaspoon sugar

¼ teaspoon salt

8 oz (225 g) cornmeal

4 fl oz (125 ml) milk

2 eggs

1 Preheat the oven to 400°F/200°C/ Gas 6. Lightly grease 14 deep muffin tins or use paper cases.

2 ▲ Fry the bacon until crisp. Drain on kitchen paper, then chop into small pieces. Set aside.

3 Gently melt the butter and margarine and set aside.

4 ▲ Sift the flour, baking powder, sugar, and salt into a large mixing bowl. Stir in the cornmeal, then make a well in the centre.

5 In a saucepan, heat the milk to lukewarm. In a small bowl, lightly whisk the eggs, then add to the milk. Stir in the melted fats.

6 ▼ Pour the milk mixture into the centre of the well and stir until smooth and well blended.

7 ▲ Stir the bacon into the mixture, then spoon the mixture into the prepared cups, filling them half-full. Bake until risen and lightly coloured, about 20 minutes. Serve hot or warm.

Corn Bread

MAKES 1 LOAF

4 oz (115 g) plain flour
2½ oz (75 g) caster sugar
1 tsp salt
1 tbsp baking powder
6 oz (170 g) cornmeal, or polenta
12 fl oz (350 ml) milk
2 eggs
3 oz (85 g) butter, melted
4 oz (115 g) margarine, melted

1 Preheat a 400°F/200°C/Gas 6 oven. Line a 9 × 5 in (23 × 13 cm) loaf tin with greaseproof paper and grease.

2 Sift the flour, sugar, salt and baking powder into a mixing bowl.

3 ▼ Add the cornmeal and stir to blend. Make a well in the centre.

4 ▲ Whisk together the milk, eggs, butter and margarine. Pour the mixture into the well. Stir until just blended; do not overmix.

5 Pour into the tin and bake until a skewer inserted in the centre comes out clean, about 45 minutes. Serve hot or at room temperature.

Spicy Sweetcorn Bread

MAKES 9 SQUARES

3–4 whole canned chilli peppers, drained
2 eggs
16 fl oz (450 ml) buttermilk
2 oz (55 g) butter, melted
2 oz (55 g) plain flour
1 tsp bicarbonate of soda
2 tsp salt
6 oz (170 g) cornmeal, or polenta
12 oz (350 g) canned sweetcorn or frozen sweetcorn, thawed

1 Preheat a 400°F/200°C/Gas 6 oven. Line the bottom and sides of a 9 in (23 cm) square cake tin with greaseproof paper and grease lightly.

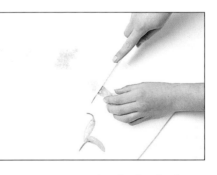

2 ▲ With a sharp knife, finely chop the chillis and set aside.

3 ▲ In a large bowl, whisk the eggs until frothy, then whisk in the buttermilk. Add the melted butter.

4 In another large bowl, sift together the flour, bicarbonate of soda and salt. Fold into the buttermilk mixture in 3 batches, then fold in the cornmeal in 3 batches.

5 ▲ Fold in the chillis and sweetcorn.

6 Pour the mixture into the prepared tin and bake until a skewer inserted in the middle comes out clean, 25–30 minutes. Let stand for 2–3 minutes before unmoulding. Cut into squares and serve warm.

Corn Bread (top), Spicy Sweetcorn Bread

Fruity Tea Bread

MAKES 1 LOAF

8 oz (225 g) plain flour
4 oz (115 g) caster sugar
1 tbsp baking powder
½ tsp salt
grated rind of 1 large orange
5½ fl oz (170 ml) fresh orange juice
2 eggs, lightly beaten
3 oz (85 g) butter or margarine, melted
4 oz (115 g) fresh cranberries, or bilberries
2 oz (55 g) chopped walnuts

1 Preheat a 350°F/180°C/Gas 4 oven. Line a 9 × 5 in (23 × 13 cm) loaf tin with greaseproof paper and grease.

2 Sift the flour, sugar, baking powder and salt into a mixing bowl.

3 ▼ Stir in the orange rind.

4 ▲ Make a well in the centre and add the orange juice, eggs and melted butter or margarine. Stir from the centre until the ingredients are blended; do not overmix.

5 ▲ Add the berries and walnuts and stir until blended.

6 Transfer the mixture to the prepared tin and bake until a skewer inserted in the centre comes out clean, 45–50 minutes.

7 ▲ Let cool in the tin for 10 minutes before transferring to a rack to cool completely. Serve thinly sliced, toasted or plain, with butter or cream cheese and jam.

Date and Pecan Loaf

MAKES 1 LOAF

6 oz (170 g) stoned dates, chopped
6 fl oz (175 ml) boiling water
2 oz (55 g) unsalted butter, at room temperature
2 oz (55 g) dark brown sugar
2 oz (55 g) caster sugar
1 egg, at room temperature
2 tbsp brandy
5½ oz (165 g) plain flour
2 tsp baking powder
½ tsp salt
¾ tsp freshly grated nutmeg
3 oz (85 g) coarsely chopped pecans or walnuts

1 ▲ Place the dates in a bowl and pour over the boiling water. Set aside to cool.

2 Preheat a 350°F/180°C/Gas 4 oven. Line a 9 × 5 in (23 × 13 cm) loaf tin with greaseproof paper and grease.

3 ▲ With an electric mixer, cream the butter and sugars until light and fluffy. Beat in the egg and brandy, then set aside.

4 Sift the flour, baking powder, salt and nutmeg together, 3 times.

5 ▼ Fold the dry ingredients into the sugar mixture in 3 batches, alternating with the dates and water.

6 ▲ Fold in the nuts.

7 Pour the mixture into the prepared tin and bake until a skewer inserted in the centre comes out clean, 45–50 minutes. Let cool in the tin for 10 minutes before transferring to a rack to cool completely.

Orange and Honey Tea Bread

MAKES 1 LOAF

13½ oz (385 g) plain flour

2½ teaspoons baking powder

½ teaspoon bicarbonate of soda

½ teaspoon salt

1 oz (30 g) margarine

8 fl oz (250 ml) clear honey

1 egg, at room temperature, lightly beaten

1½ tablespoons grated orange rind

6 fl oz (175 ml) freshly squeezed orange juice

4 oz (115 g) walnuts, chopped

1 Preheat a 325°F/170°C/Gas 3 oven.

2 Sift together the flour, baking powder, bicarbonate of soda and salt.

3 Line the bottom and sides of a 9 × 5 in (23 × 13 cm) loaf tin with greaseproof paper and grease.

4 ▲ With an electric mixer, cream the margarine until soft. Stir in the honey until blended, then stir in the egg. Add the orange rind and stir to combine thoroughly.

5 ▲ Fold the flour mixture into the honey and egg mixture in 3 batches, alternating with the orange juice. Stir in the walnuts.

6 Pour into the tin and bake until a skewer inserted in the centre comes out clean, 60–70 minutes. Let stand 10 minutes before turning out onto a rack to cool.

Apple Loaf

MAKES 1 LOAF

1 egg

8 fl oz (250 ml) bottled or homemade apple sauce

2 oz (55 g) butter or margarine, melted

3¾ oz (110 g) dark brown sugar

1¾ oz (50 g) caster sugar

10 oz (285 g) plain flour

2 teaspoons baking powder

½ teaspoon bicarbonate of soda

½ teaspoon salt

1 teaspoon ground cinnamon

½ teaspoon grated nutmeg

2½ oz (70 g) currants or raisins

2 oz (55 g) pecans or walnuts, chopped

1 Preheat a 350°F/180°C/Gas 4 oven. Line a 9 × 5 in (23 × 13 cm) loaf tin with greaseproof paper and grease.

2 ▲ Break the egg into a bowl and beat lightly. Stir in the apple sauce, butter or margarine and both sugars. Set aside.

3 In another bowl, sift together the flour, baking powder, bicarbonate of soda, salt, cinnamon and nutmeg. Fold dry ingredients into the apple sauce mixture in 3 batches.

4 ▼ Stir in the currants or raisins, and nuts.

5 Pour into the prepared tin and bake until a skewer inserted in the centre comes out clean, about 1 hour. Let stand 10 minutes. Turn out onto a rack and cool completely.

Orange and Honey Tea Bread (top), Apple Loaf

Lemon and Walnut Tea Bread

MAKES 1 LOAF

4 oz (115 g) butter or margarine, at room
temperature

3½ oz (100 g) sugar

2 eggs, at room temperature, separated

grated rind of 2 lemons

2 tablespoons lemon juice

7½ oz (215 g) plain flour

2 teaspoons baking powder

4 fl oz (125 ml) milk

2 oz (55 g) walnuts, chopped

⅛ teaspoon salt

1 Preheat a 350°F/180°C/Gas 4 oven.
Line a 9 × 5 in (23 × 13 cm) loaf tin
with greaseproof paper and grease.

2 With an electric mixer, cream the
butter or margarine with the sugar
until light and fluffy.

3 ▲ Beat in the egg yolks.

4 Add the lemon rind and juice and
stir until blended. Set aside.

5 ▲ In another bowl, sift together
the flour and baking powder, 3 times.
Fold into the butter mixture in 3
batches, alternating with the milk.
Fold in the walnuts. Set aside.

6 ▲ Beat the egg whites and salt
until stiff peaks form. Fold a large
dollop of the egg whites into the
walnut mixture to lighten it. Fold in
the remaining egg whites carefully
until just blended.

7 ▲ Pour the batter into the
prepared tin and bake until a skewer
inserted in the centre of the loaf
comes out clean, 45–50 minutes. Let
stand 5 minutes before turning out
onto a rack to cool completely.

Apricot Nut Loaf

MAKES 1 LOAF

4 oz (115 g) dried apricots
1 large orange
3 oz (85 g) raisins
5 oz (140 g) caster sugar
3 fl oz (85 ml) oil
2 eggs, lightly beaten
9 oz (250 g) plain flour
2 tsp baking powder
½ tsp salt
1 tsp bicarbonate of soda
2 oz (55 g) chopped walnuts

1 Preheat a 350°F/180°C/Gas 4 oven. Line a 9 × 5 in (23 × 13 cm) loaf tin with greaseproof paper and grease.

2 Place the apricots in a bowl, cover with lukewarm water and leave to stand for 30 minutes.

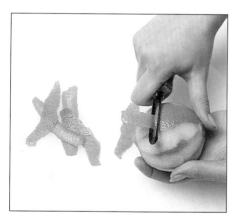

3 ▲ With a vegetable peeler, remove the orange rind, leaving the pith.

4 With a sharp knife, finely chop the orange rind strips.

5 Drain the apricots and chop coarsely. Place in a bowl with the orange rind and raisins. Set aside.

6 Squeeze the peeled orange. Measure the juice and add enough hot water to obtain 6 fl oz (175 ml) liquid.

7 ▼ Pour the orange juice mixture over the apricot mixture. Stir in the sugar, oil and eggs. Set aside.

8 In another bowl, sift together the flour, baking powder, salt and bicarbonate of soda. Fold the flour mixture into the apricot mixture in 3 batches.

9 ▲ Stir in the walnuts.

10 Spoon the mixture into the prepared tin and bake until a skewer inserted in the centre comes out clean, 55–60 minutes. If the loaf browns too quickly, protect the top with a sheet of foil. Let cool in the pan for 10 minutes before transferring to a rack to cool completely.

Mango Tea Bread

MAKES 2 LOAVES

10 oz (285 g) plain flour
2 teaspoons bicarbonate of soda
2 teaspoons ground cinnamon
½ teaspoon salt
4 oz (115 g) margarine, at room temperature
3 eggs, at room temperature
10½ oz (300 g) sugar
4 fl oz (125 ml) vegetable oil
1 large ripe mango, peeled and chopped
3¼ oz (90 g) desiccated coconut
2½ oz (70 g) raisins

1 Preheat the oven to 350°F/180°C/ Gas 4. Line the bottom and sides of 2 9 × 5 in (23 × 13 cm) loaf tins with greaseproof paper and grease.

2 Sift together the flour, bicarbonate of soda, cinnamon and salt. Set aside.

3 With an electric mixer, cream the margarine until soft.

4 ▼ Beat in the eggs and sugar until light and fluffy. Beat in the oil.

5 Fold the dry ingredients into the creamed ingredients in 3 batches.

6 Fold in the mangoes, two-thirds of the coconut and the raisins.

7 ▲ Spoon the batter into the pans.

8 Sprinkle over the remaining coconut. Bake until a skewer inserted in the centre comes out clean, 50–60 minutes. Let stand for 10 minutes before turning out onto a rack to cool completely.

Courgette Tea Bread

MAKES 1 LOAF

2 oz (55 g) butter
3 eggs
8 fl oz (250 ml) vegetable oil
10½ oz (300 g) sugar
2 medium unpeeled courgettes, grated
10 oz (285 g) plain flour
2 teaspoons bicarbonate of soda
1 teaspoon baking powder
1 teaspoon salt
1 teaspoon ground cinnamon
1 teaspoon grated nutmeg
¼ teaspoon ground cloves
4 oz (115 g) walnuts, chopped

1 Preheat the oven to 350°F/180°C/ Gas 4.

2 Line the bottom and sides of a 9 × 5 in (23 × 13 cm) loaf tin with greaseproof paper and grease.

3 ▲ In a saucepan, melt the butter over low heat. Set aside.

4 With an electric mixer, beat the eggs and oil together until thick. Beat in the sugar. Stir in the melted butter and courgettes. Set aside.

5 ▲ In another bowl, sift all the dry ingredients together 3 times. Carefully fold into the courgette mixture. Fold in the walnuts.

6 Pour into the tin and bake until a skewer inserted in the centre comes out clean, 60–70 minutes. Let stand 10 minutes before turning out onto wire rack to cool completely.

Mango Tea Bread (top), Courgette Tea Bread

Wholewheat Banana Nut Loaf

MAKES 1 LOAF

| 4 oz (115 g) butter, at room temperature |
| 4 oz (115 g) caster sugar |
| 2 eggs, at room temperature |
| 4 oz (115 g) plain flour |
| 1 tsp bicarbonate of soda |
| ¼ tsp salt |
| 1 tsp ground cinnamon |
| 2 oz (55 g) wholewheat flour |
| 3 large ripe bananas |
| 1 tsp vanilla essence |
| 2 oz (55 g) chopped walnuts |

1 Preheat a 350°F/180°C/Gas 4 oven. Line the bottom and sides of a 9 × 5 in (23 × 13 cm) loaf tin with greaseproof paper and grease the paper.

2 With an electric mixer, cream the butter and sugar together until light and fluffy.

3 ▲ Add the eggs, 1 at a time, beating well after each addition.

4 Sift the plain flour, bicarbonate of soda, salt and cinnamon over the butter mixture and stir to blend.

5 ▲ Stir in the wholewheat flour.

6 ▲ With a fork, mash the bananas to a purée, then stir into the mixture. Stir in the vanilla and nuts.

7 ▲ Pour the mixture into the prepared tin and spread level.

8 Bake until a skewer inserted in the centre comes out clean, 50–60 minutes. Let stand 10 minutes before transferring to a rack.

Dried Fruit Loaf

MAKES 1 LOAF

1 lb (450 g) mixed dried fruit, such as currants, raisins, chopped dried apricots and dried cherries

10 fl oz (300 ml) cold strong tea

7 oz (200 g) dark brown sugar

grated rind and juice of 1 small orange

grated rind and juice of 1 lemon

1 egg, lightly beaten

7 oz (200 g) plain flour

1 tbsp baking powder

⅛ tsp salt

1 ▲ In a bowl, mix the dried fruit with the tea and soak overnight.

2 Preheat a 350°F/180°C/Gas 4 oven. Line the bottom and sides of a 9 × 5 in (23 × 13 cm) loaf tin with greaseproof paper and grease the paper.

3 ▲ Strain the fruit, reserving the liquid. In a bowl, combine the sugar, orange and lemon rind, and fruit.

4 ▼ Pour the orange and lemon juice into a measuring jug; if the quantity is less than 8 fl oz (250 ml), top up with the soaking liquid.

5 Stir the citrus juices and egg into the dried fruit mixture.

6 In another bowl, sift together the flour, baking powder and salt. Stir into the fruit mixture until blended.

7 Transfer to the prepared tin and bake until a skewer inserted in the centre comes out clean, about 1¼ hours. Let stand 10 minutes before unmoulding.

Bilberry Tea Bread

MAKES 8 PIECES

2 oz (55 g) butter or margarine, at room temperature

6 oz (170 g) caster sugar

1 egg, at room temperature

4 fl oz (125 ml) milk

8 oz (225 g) plain flour

2 tsp baking powder

½ tsp salt

10 oz (285 g) fresh bilberries, or blueberries

FOR THE TOPPING

4 oz (115 g) sugar

1½ oz (45 g) plain flour

½ tsp ground cinnamon

2 oz (55 g) butter, cut in pieces

1 Preheat a 375°F/190°C/Gas 5 oven. Grease a 9 in (23 cm) baking dish.

2 With an electric mixer, cream the butter or margarine with the sugar until light and fluffy. Add the egg, beat to combine, then mix in the milk until blended.

3 ▼ Sift over the flour, baking powder and salt and stir just enough to blend the ingredients.

4 ▲ Add the berries and stir.

5 Transfer to the baking dish.

6 ▲ For the topping, place the sugar, flour, cinnamon and butter in a mixing bowl. Cut in with a pastry blender until the mixture resembles coarse breadcrumbs.

7 ▲ Sprinkle the topping over the mixture in the baking dish.

8 Bake until a skewer inserted in the centre comes out clean, about 45 minutes. Serve warm or cold.

Chocolate Chip Walnut Loaf

MAKES 1 LOAF

3½ oz (100 g) caster sugar
3½ oz (100 g) flour
1 teaspoon baking powder
4 tablespoons cornflour
4½ oz (130 g) butter, at room temperature
2 eggs, at room temperature
1 teaspoon vanilla extract
2 tablespoons currants or raisins
1 oz (30 g) walnuts, finely chopped
grated rind of ½ lemon
3 tablespoons plain chocolate chips
icing sugar, for dusting

1 Preheat the oven to 350°F/180°C/ Gas 4. Grease and line an 8½ × 4½ in (22 × 12 cm) loaf tin.

2 ▲ Sprinkle 1½ tablespoons of the caster sugar into the pan and tilt to distribute the sugar in an even layer over the bottom and sides. Shake out any excess.

3 ▼ Sift together the flour, baking powder and cornflour into a mixing bowl, 3 times. Set aside.

4 With an electric mixer, cream the butter until soft. Add the remaining sugar and continue beating until light and fluffy. Add the eggs, 1 at a time, beating to incorporate thoroughly after each addition.

5 Gently fold the dry ingredients into the butter mixture, in 3 batches; do not overmix.

6 ▲ Fold in the vanilla, currants or raisins, walnuts, lemon rind, and chocolate chips until just blended.

7 Pour the mixture into the prepared tin and bake until a cake tester inserted in the centre comes out clean, 45–50 minutes. Let cool in the tin for 5 minutes before transferring to a rack to cool completely. Dust over an even layer of icing sugar before serving.

Glazed Banana Spice Loaf

MAKES 1 LOAF

1 large ripe banana
4 oz (115 g) butter, at room temperature
5½ oz (150 g) caster sugar
2 eggs, at room temperature
7½ oz (215 g) plain flour
1 teaspoon salt
1 teaspoon bicarbonate of soda
½ teaspoon grated nutmeg
¼ teaspoon ground allspice
¼ teaspoon ground cloves
6 fl oz (175 ml) soured cream
1 teaspoon vanilla essence

FOR THE GLAZE

4 oz (115 g) icing sugar
1–2 tablespoons lemon juice

1 Preheat a 350°F/180°C/Gas 4 oven. Line an 8½ × 4½ in (21.5 × 11.5 cm) loaf tin with greaseproof and grease.

2 ▼ With a fork, mash the banana in a bowl. Set aside.

3 With an electric mixer, cream the butter and sugar until light and fluffy. Add the eggs, 1 at a time, beating to blend well after each addition.

4 Sift together the flour, salt, bicarbonate of soda, nutmeg, allspice and cloves. Add to the butter mixture and stir to combine well.

5 ▲ Add the soured cream, banana, and vanilla and mix just enough to blend. Pour into the prepared tin.

6 ▲ Bake until the top springs back when touched lightly, 45–50 minutes. Let cool in the pan for 10 minutes. Turn out onto wire rack to cool.

7 ▲ For the glaze, combine the icing sugar and lemon juice, then stir until smooth.

8 To glaze, place the cooled loaf on a rack set over a baking sheet. Pour the glaze over the top of the loaf and allow to set.

Sweet Sesame Loaf

MAKES 1 OR 2 LOAVES

3 oz (85 g) sesame seeds

10 oz (285 g) plain flour

2½ teaspoons baking powder

1 teaspoon salt

2 oz (55 g) butter or margarine, at room temperature

4½ oz (125 g) sugar

2 eggs, at room temperature

grated rind of 1 lemon

12 fl oz (350 ml) milk

1 Preheat a 350°F/180°C/Gas 4 oven. Line a 9 × 5 in (23 × 13 cm) loaf tin with greaseproof paper and grease.

2 ▲ Reserve 2 tablespoons of the sesame seeds. Spread the rest on a baking sheet and bake until lightly toasted, about 10 minutes.

3 Sift the flour, salt and baking powder into a bowl.

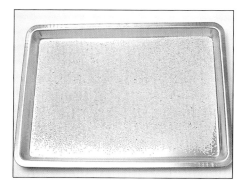

4 ▲ Stir in the toasted sesame seeds and set aside.

5 With an electric mixer, cream the butter or margarine and sugar together until light and fluffy. Beat in the eggs, then stir in the lemon rind and milk.

6 ▼ Pour the milk mixture over the dry ingredients and fold in with a large metal spoon until just blended.

7 ▲ Pour into the tin and sprinkle over the reserved sesame seeds.

8 Bake until a skewer inserted in the centre comes out clean, about 1 hour. Let cool in the tin for 10 minutes. Turn out onto wire rack to cool completely.

Wholemeal Scones

MAKES 16

6 oz (170 g) cold butter

12 oz (350 g) wholemeal flour

5 oz (140 g) plain flour

2 tablespoons sugar

½ teaspoon salt

2½ teaspoons bicarbonate of soda

2 eggs

6 fl oz (175 ml) buttermilk

1¼ oz (35 g) raisins

1 Preheat the oven to 400°F/200°C/Gas 6. Grease and flour a large baking sheet.

2 ▲ Cut the butter into small pieces.

3 Combine the dry ingredients in a bowl. Add the butter and rub in with your fingertips until the mixture resembles coarse breadcrumbs. Set aside.

4 In another bowl, whisk together the eggs and buttermilk. Set aside 2 tablespoons for glazing.

5 Stir the remaining egg mixture into the dry ingredients until it just holds together. Stir in the raisins.

6 Roll out the dough about ¾ in (2 cm) thick. Stamp out circles with a biscuit cutter. Place on the prepared sheet and brush with the glaze.

7 Bake until golden, 12–15 minutes. Allow to cool slightly before serving. Split in two with a fork while still warm and spread with butter and jam, if wished.

Orange and Raisin Scones

MAKES 16

10 oz (285 g) plain flour

1½ tablespoons baking powder

2¼ oz (60 g) sugar

½ teaspoon salt

2½ g (70 g) butter, diced

2½ g (70 g) margarine, diced

grated rind of 1 large orange

2 oz (55 g) raisins

4 fl oz (125 ml) buttermilk

milk, for glazing

1 Preheat the oven to 425°F/220°C/Gas 7. Grease and flour a large baking sheet.

2 Combine the dry ingredients in a large bowl. Add the butter and margarine and rub in with your fingertips until the mixture resembles coarse breadcrumbs.

3 ▲ Add the orange rind and raisins.

4 Gradually stir in the buttermilk to form a soft dough.

5 ▲ Roll out the dough about ¾ in (2 cm) thick. Stamp out circles with a biscuit cutter.

6 ▲ Place on the prepared sheet and brush the tops with milk.

7 Bake until golden, 12–15 minutes. Serve hot or warm, with butter, or whipped or clotted cream, and jam.

~ COOK'S TIP ~

For light tender scones, handle the dough as little as possible. If you wish, split the scones when cool and toast them under a preheated grill. Butter them while still hot.

Wholemeal Scones (top), Orange and Raisin Scones

Buttermilk Scones

MAKES 15

7 oz (200 g) plain flour

1 teaspoon salt

1 teaspoon baking powder

½ teaspoon bicarbonate of soda

4 tablespoons cold butter or margarine

6 fl oz (175 ml) buttermilk

1 Preheat the oven to 425°F/220°C/ Gas 7. Grease a baking sheet.

2 Sift the dry ingredients into a bowl. Rub in the butter or margarine with your fingertips until the mixture resembles breadcrumbs.

3 ▼ Gradually pour in the buttermilk, stirring with a fork to form a soft dough.

4 ▲ Roll out the dough until about ½ in (1 cm) thick. Stamp out rounds with a 2-inch (5 cm) biscuit cutter.

5 Place on the prepared baking sheet and bake until golden, 12–15 minutes. Serve warm or at room temperature.

Traditional Sweet Scones

MAKES 8

6 oz (170 g) flour

2 tablespoons sugar

3 teaspoons baking powder

⅛ teaspoon salt

5 tablespoons cold butter, cut in pieces

4 fl oz (125 ml) milk

1 Preheat the oven to 425°F/220°C/ Gas 7. Grease a baking sheet.

2 ▲ Sift the flour, sugar, baking powder, and salt into a bowl.

3 Cut in the butter with a pastry blender until the mixture resembles coarse crumbs.

4 Pour in the milk and stir with a fork to form a soft dough.

5 ▲ Roll out the dough about ¼ in (½ cm) thick. Stamp out rounds using a 2½ in (6 cm) biscuit cutter.

6 Place on the prepared sheet and bake until golden, about 12 minutes. Serve hot or warm, with butter and jam, to accompany tea or coffee.

> **~ VARIATION ~**
>
> To make a delicious and speedy dessert, split the scones in half while still warm. Butter one half, top with lightly sugared fresh strawberries, raspberries or blueberries, and sandwich with the other half. Serve at once with dollops of whipped cream.

Herb Popovers

MAKES 12

3 eggs

8 fl oz (250 ml) milk

1 oz (30 g) butter, melted

3 oz (85 g) plain flour

⅛ tsp salt

1 small sprig each mixed fresh herbs, such as chives, tarragon, dill and parsley

1 Preheat a 425°F/220°C/Gas 7 oven. Grease 12 small ramekins or individual baking cups.

2 With an electric mixer, beat the eggs until blended. Beat in the milk and melted butter.

3 Sift together the flour and salt, then beat into the egg mixture to combine thoroughly.

4 ▼ Strip the herb leaves from the stems and chop finely. Mix together and measure out 2 tablespoons. Stir the herbs into the batter.

5 ▲ Fill the prepared cups half-full.

6 Bake until golden, 25–30 minutes. Do not open the oven door during baking time or the popovers may collapse. For drier popovers, pierce each one with a knife after the 30 minute baking time and bake for 5 minutes more. Serve hot.

Cheese Popovers

MAKES 12

3 eggs

8 fl oz (250 ml) milk

1 oz (30 g) butter, melted

3 oz (85 g) plain flour

¼ tsp salt

¼ tsp paprika

1 oz (30 g) freshly grated Parmesan cheese

~ **VARIATION** ~

For traditional Yorkshire Pudding, omit the cheese and paprika, and use 4–6 tablespoons of beef dripping to replace the butter. Put them into the oven in time to serve warm as an accompaniment for roast beef.

1 Preheat a 425°F/220°C/Gas 7 oven. Grease 12 small ramekins.

2 ▲ With an electric mixer, beat the eggs until blended. Beat in the milk and melted butter.

3 ▲ Sift together the flour, salt and paprika, then beat into the egg mixture. Add the cheese and stir.

4 Fill the prepared cups half-full and bake until golden, 25–30 minutes. Do not open the oven door or the popovers may collapse. For drier popovers, pierce each one with a knife after the 30 minute baking time and bake for 5 minutes more. Serve hot.

Herb Popovers (top), Cheese Popovers

YEAST BREADS

~

Though the pace of today's life leaves little time for baking,
breadmaking can be very therapeutic. The process is simple
yet infinitely variable, as the loaves that follow prove.
Roll up your sleeves and create a tradition.

White Bread

MAKES 2 LOAVES

2 fl oz (65 ml) lukewarm water

1 tablespoon active dried yeast

2 tablespoons sugar

16 fl oz (450 ml) lukewarm milk

1 oz (30 g) butter or margarine, at room temperature

2 teaspoons salt

1 lb 14 oz–2 lbs (850–900 g) strong flour

1 Combine the water, yeast and 1 tablespoon of sugar in a measuring jug and let stand for 15 minutes until the mixture is frothy.

2 ▼ Pour the milk into a large bowl. Add the remaining sugar, the butter or margarine, and salt. Stir in the yeast mixture.

3 Stir in the flour, 5 oz (140 g) at a time, until a stiff dough is obtained. Alternatively, use a food processor.

4 ▲ Transfer the dough to a floured surface. To knead, push the dough away from you with the palm of your hand, then fold it towards you, and push it away again. Repeat until the dough is smooth and elastic.

5 Place the dough in a large greased bowl, cover with a plastic bag, and leave to rise in a warm place until doubled in volume, 2–3 hours.

6 Grease 2 9 × 5 in (23 × 13 cm) tins.

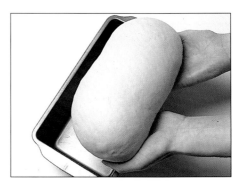

7 ▲ Punch down the risen dough with your fist and divide in half. Form into a loaf shape and place in the tins, seam-side down. Cover and let rise in a warm place until almost doubled in volume, about 45 minutes.

8 Preheat a 375°F/190°C/Gas 5 oven.

9 Bake until firm and brown, 45–50 minutes. Turn out and tap the bottom of a loaf: if it sounds hollow the loaf is done. If necessary, return to the oven and bake a few minutes more.

10 Let cool on a rack.

Country Bread

MAKES 2 LOAVES

12 oz (350 g) wholewheat flour
12 oz (350 g) plain flour
5 oz (140 g) strong plain flour
4 tsp salt
2 oz (55 g) butter, at room temperature
16 fl oz (450 ml) lukewarm milk
FOR THE STARTER
1 tbsp active dry yeast
8 fl oz (250 ml) lukewarm water
5 oz (140 g) plain flour
¼ tsp caster sugar

1 ▲ For the starter, combine the yeast, water, flour and sugar in a bowl and stir with a fork. Cover and leave in a warm place for 2–3 hours, or leave overnight in a cool place.

2 Place the flours, salt and butter in a food processor and process just until blended, 1–2 minutes.

3 Stir together the milk and starter, then slowly pour into the processor, with the motor running, until the mixture forms a dough. If necessary, add more water. Alternatively, the dough can be mixed by hand. Transfer to a floured surface and knead until smooth and elastic.

4 Place in an ungreased bowl, cover with a plastic bag, and leave to rise in a warm place until doubled in volume, about 1½ hours.

5 Transfer to a floured surface and knead briefly. Return to the bowl and leave to rise until tripled in volume, about 1½ hours.

6 ▲ Divide the dough in half. Cut off one-third of the dough from each half and shape into balls. Shape the larger remaining portion of each half into balls. Grease a baking sheet.

7 ▲ For each loaf, top the large ball with the small ball and press the centre with the handle of a wooden spoon to secure. Cover with a plastic bag, slash the top, and leave to rise.

8 Preheat a 400°F/200°C/Gas 6 oven. Dust the dough with flour and bake until the top is browned and the bottom sounds hollow when tapped, 45–50 minutes. Cool on a rack.

Plaited Loaf

MAKES 1 LOAF

1 tablespoon active dried yeast
1 teaspoon honey
8 fl oz (250 ml) lukewarm milk
2 oz (55 g) butter, melted
15 oz (420 g) strong flour
1 teaspoon salt
1 egg, lightly beaten
1 egg yolk beaten with 1 teaspoon milk, for glazing

1 ▼ Combine the yeast, honey, milk and butter. Stir and leave for 15 minutes to dissolve.

2 In a large bowl, mix together the flour and salt. Make a well in the centre and add the yeast mixture and egg. With a wooden spoon, stir from the centre, incorporating flour with each turn, to obtain a rough dough.

3 Transfer to a floured surface and knead until smooth and elastic. Place in a clean bowl, cover and leave to rise in a warm place until doubled in volume, about 1½ hours.

4 Grease a baking sheet. Punch down the dough and divide into three equal pieces. Roll to shape each piece into a long thin strip.

5 ▲ Begin plaiting with the centre strip, tucking in the ends. Cover loosely and leave to rise in a warm place for 30 minutes.

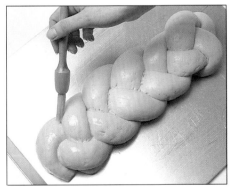

6 ▲ Preheat a 375°F/190°C/Gas 5 oven. Place the bread in a cool place while the oven heats. Brush with the glaze and bake until golden, 40–45 minutes. Turn out onto a rack to cool.

Sesame Seed Bread

MAKES 1 LOAF

2 tsp active dry yeast
10 fl oz (300 ml) lukewarm water
7 oz (200 g) plain flour
7 oz (200 g) wholewheat flour
2 tsp salt
2½ oz (70 g) toasted sesame seeds
milk, for glazing
2 tbsp sesame seeds, for sprinkling

1 Combine the yeast and 5 tbsp of the water and leave to dissolve. Mix the flours and salt in a large bowl. Make a well in the centre and pour in the yeast and water.

2 ▲ With a wooden spoon, stir from the centre, incorporating flour with each turn, to obtain a rough dough.

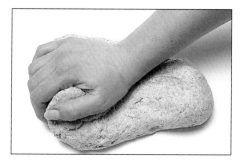

3 ▲ Transfer to a floured surface. To knead, push the dough away from you with the palm of your hand, then fold it towards you and push away again. Repeat until smooth and elastic, then return to the bowl and cover with a plastic bag. Leave in a warm place until doubled in volume, 1½–2 hours.

4 ▲ Grease a 9 in (23 cm) cake tin. Punch down the dough and knead in the sesame seeds. Divide the dough into 16 balls and place in the pan. Cover with a plastic bag and leave in a warm place until risen above the rim of the tin.

5 ▼ Preheat a 425°F/220°C/Gas 7 oven. Brush the loaf with milk and sprinkle with the sesame seeds. Bake for 15 minutes. Lower the heat to 375°F/190°C/Gas 5 and bake until the bottom sounds hollow when tapped, about 30 minutes more. Cool on a rack.

Wholewheat Bread

MAKES 1 LOAF

1 lb 5 oz (600 g) wholewheat flour

2 tsp salt

4 tsp active dry yeast

15 fl oz (425 ml) lukewarm water

2 tbsp honey

3 tbsp oil

1½ oz (45 g) wheatgerm

milk, for glazing

1 Combine the flour and salt in a bowl and place in the oven at its lowest setting until warmed, 8–10 minutes.

2 Meanwhile, combine the yeast with half of the water in a small bowl and leave to dissolve.

3 ▼ Make a well in the centre of the flour. Pour in the yeast mixture, the remaining water, honey, oil and wheatgerm. With a wooden spoon, stir from the centre until smooth.

4 Transfer the dough to a lightly floured surface and knead just enough to shape into a loaf.

5 ▲ Grease a 9 × 5 in (23 × 13 cm) loaf tin, place the dough in it and cover with a plastic bag. Leave in a warm place until the dough is about 1 in (2.5 cm) higher than the tin rim, about 1 hour.

6 Preheat a 400°F/200°C/Gas 6 oven. Bake until the bottom sounds hollow when tapped, 35–40 minutes. Cool.

Rye Bread

MAKES 1 LOAF

7 oz (200 g) rye flour

16 fl oz (450 ml) boiling water

4 fl oz (125 ml) black treacle

2½ oz (70 g) butter, cut in pieces

1 tbsp salt

2 tbsp caraway seeds

1 tbsp active dry yeast

4 fl oz (125 ml) lukewarm water

about 1 lb 14 oz (850 g) plain flour

semolina or flour, for dusting

~ **COOK'S TIP** ~

To bring out the flavour of the caraway seeds, toast them lightly. Spread the seeds on a baking tray and place in a preheated 325°F/170°C/ Gas 3 oven for about 7 minutes.

1 ▲ Mix the rye flour, boiling water, treacle, butter, salt and caraway seeds in a large bowl. Leave to cool.

2 In another bowl, mix the yeast and lukewarm water and leave to dissolve. Stir into the rye flour mixture. Stir in just enough plain flour to obtain a stiff dough. If it becomes too stiff, stir with your hands.

3 Transfer to a floured surface and knead until the dough is no longer sticky and is smooth and shiny.

4 Place in a greased bowl, cover with a plastic bag, and leave in a warm place until doubled in volume. Punch down the dough, cover, and let rise again for 30 minutes.

5 Preheat a 350°F/180°C/Gas 4 oven. Dust a baking sheet with semolina.

6 ▼ Shape the dough into a ball. Place on the sheet and score several times across the top. Bake until the bottom sounds hollow when tapped, about 40 minutes. Cool on a rack.

Wholewheat Bread (top), Rye Bread

Buttermilk Graham Bread

SERVES 8

2 teaspoons active dried yeast

4 fl oz (120 ml) lukewarm water

8 oz (225 g) graham or wholewheat
flour

12 oz (350 g) plain flour

4½ oz (130 g) cornmeal

2 teaspoons salt

2 tablespoons sugar

4 tablespoons butter, at room
temperature

16 fl oz (475 ml) lukewarm
buttermilk

1 beaten egg, for glazing

sesame seeds, for sprinkling

1 Combine the yeast and water, stir,
and leave for 15 minutes to dissolve.

2 ▲ Mix together the two flours,
cornmeal, salt and sugar in a large
bowl. Make a well in the centre and
pour in the yeast mixture, then add
the butter and the buttermilk.

3 ▲ Stir from the centre, mixing in
the flour until a rough dough is
formed. If too stiff, use your hands.

4 ▲ Transfer to a floured surface
and knead until smooth. Place in a
clean bowl, cover, and leave in a
warm place for 2–3 hours.

5 ▲ Grease 2 8 in (20 cm) square
baking tins. Punch down the dough.
Divide into eight pieces and roll
them into balls. Place four in each
tin. Cover and leave in a warm place
for about 1 hour.

6 Preheat the oven to 375°F/190°C/
Gas 5. Brush with the glaze, then
sprinkle over the sesame seeds. Bake
for about 50 minutes, or until the
bottoms sound hollow when tapped.
Cool on a wire rack.

Multi-Grain Bread

MAKES 2 LOAVES

1 tablespoon active dried yeast
2 fl oz (65 ml) lukewarm water
2½ oz (70 g) rolled oats (not quick cooking)
16 fl oz (450 ml) milk
2 teaspoons salt
2 fl oz (65 ml) oil
2 oz (55 g) light brown sugar
2 tablespoons honey
2 eggs, lightly beaten
1 oz (30 g) wheat germ
6 oz (170 g) soya flour
12 oz (350 g) wholemeal flour
15 oz–1 lb 1½ oz (420–490 g) strong flour

1 Combine the yeast and water, stir, and leave for 15 minutes to dissolve.

2 ▲ Place the oats in a large bowl. Scald the milk, then pour over the rolled oats.

3 Stir in the salt, oil, sugar and honey. Leave until lukewarm.

> ~ **VARIATION** ~
>
> Different flours may be used in this recipe, such as rye, barley, buckwheat or cornmeal. Try replacing the wheat germ and the soya flour with one or two of these, using the same total amount.

4 ▲ Stir in the yeast mixture, eggs, wheat germ, soya and wholemeal flours. Gradually stir in enough strong flour to obtain a rough dough.

5 Transfer the dough to a floured surface and knead, adding flour if necessary, until smooth and elastic. Return to a clean bowl, cover and leave to rise in a warm place until doubled in volume, about 2½ hours.

6 Grease 2 8½ × 4½ in (21.5 × 11.5 cm) bread tins. Punch down the risen dough and knead briefly.

7 Divide the dough into quarters. Roll each quarter into a cylinder 1½ in (3 cm) thick. Twist together 2 cylinders and place in a tin; repeat for remaining cylinders.

8 Cover and leave to rise until doubled in size, about 1 hour.

9 Preheat a 375°F/190°C/Gas 5 oven.

10 ▲ Bake until the bottoms sound hollow when tapped lightly, 45–50 minutes. Cool on a rack.

Potato Bread

MAKES 2 LOAVES

4 tsp active dry yeast
8 fl oz (250 ml) lukewarm milk
8 oz (225 g) potatoes, boiled (reserve 8 fl oz (250 ml) of potato cooking liquid)
2 tbsp oil
4 tsp salt
1 lb 14 oz–2 lb (850–900 g) plain flour

1 Combine the yeast and milk in a large bowl and leave to dissolve, about 15 minutes.

2 Meanwhile, mash the potatoes.

3 ▲ Add the potatoes, oil and salt to the yeast mixture and mix well. Stir in the reserved cooking water, then stir in the flour, in 6 separate batches, to form a stiff dough.

4 Transfer to a floured surface and knead until smooth and elastic. Return to the bowl, cover, and leave in a warm place until doubled in size, 1–1½ hours. Punch down, then leave to rise for another 40 minutes.

5 Grease 2 9 × 5 in (23 × 13 cm) loaf tins. Roll the dough into 20 small balls. Place 2 rows of balls in each tin. Leave until the dough has risen above the rim of the tins.

6 Preheat a 400°F/200°C/Gas 6 oven. Bake for 10 minutes, then lower the heat to 375°F/190°C/Gas 5. Bake until the bottoms sound hollow when tapped, 40 minutes. Cool on a rack.

Irish Soda Bread

MAKES 1 LOAF

10 oz (285 g) plain flour
5 oz (140 g) wholewheat flour
1 tsp bicarbonate of soda
1 tsp salt
1 oz (30 g) butter or margarine, at room temperature
10 fl oz (300 ml) buttermilk
1 tbsp plain flour, for dusting

1 Preheat a 400°F/200°C/Gas 6 oven. Grease a baking sheet.

2 Sift the flours, bicarbonate of soda and salt together into a bowl. Make a well in the centre and add the butter or margarine and buttermilk. Working outwards from the centre, stir with a fork until a soft dough is formed.

3 ▲ With floured hands, gather the dough into a ball.

4 ▲ Transfer to a floured surface and knead for 3 minutes. Shape the dough into a large round.

5 ▲ Place on the baking sheet. Cut a cross in the top with a sharp knife.

6 ▲ Dust with flour. Bake until brown, 40–50 minutes. Transfer to a rack to cool.

Potato Bread (top), Irish Soda Bread

Anadama Bread

MAKES 2 LOAVES

2 teaspoons active dried yeast
4 tablespoons lukewarm water
2 oz (50 g) cornmeal
3 tablespoons butter or margarine
4 tablespoons molasses
6 fl oz (175 ml) boiling water
1 egg
12 oz (350 g) flour
2 tablespoons salt

1 Combine the yeast and lukewarm water, stir well, and leave for 15 minutes to dissolve.

2 ▼ Meanwhile, combine the cornmeal, butter or margarine, molasses and boiling water in a large bowl. Add the yeast, egg, and half of the flour. Stir together to blend.

3 ▲ Stir in the remaining flour and salt. When the dough becomes too stiff, stir with your hands until it comes away from the sides of the bowl. If it is too sticky, add more flour; if too stiff, add a little water.

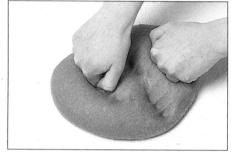

4 ▲ Transfer to a floured surface and knead until smooth and elastic. Place in a bowl, cover with a plastic bag, and leave in a warm place until doubled in size, for 2–3 hours.

5 Grease 2 7 x 3 in (18 x 7.5 cm) bread tins. Punch down the dough. Shape into two loaves and place in the tins, seam-side down. Cover and leave in a warm place for 1–2 hours.

6 ▲ Preheat the oven to 375°F/ 190°C/Gas 6. Bake for 50 minutes. Remove and cool on a wire rack.

Oatmeal Bread

MAKES 2 LOAVES

16 fl oz (450 ml) milk
1 oz (30 g) butter
2 oz (55 g) dark brown sugar
2 teaspoons salt
1 tablespoon active dried yeast
2 fl oz (65 ml) lukewarm water
13¾ oz (390 g) rolled oats (not quick-cooking)
1 lb 8 oz–1 lb 14 oz (700–850 g) strong flour

1 ▲ Scald the milk. Remove from the heat and stir in the butter, brown sugar and salt. Leave until lukewarm.

2 Combine the yeast and warm water in a large bowl and leave until the yeast is dissolved and the mixture is frothy. Stir in the milk mixture.

3 ▲ Add 10 oz (285 g) of the oats and enough flour to obtain a soft dough.

4 Transfer to a floured surface and knead until smooth and elastic.

5 ▲ Place in a greased bowl, cover with a plastic bag, and leave until doubled in volume, 2–3 hours.

6 Grease a large baking sheet. Transfer the dough to a lightly floured surface and divide in half.

7 ▼ Shape into rounds. Place on the baking sheet, cover with a tea towel and leave to rise until doubled in volume, about 1 hour.

8 Preheat a 400°F/200°C/Gas 6 oven. Score the tops and sprinkle with the remaining oats. Bake until the bottoms sound hollow when tapped, 45–50 minutes. Cool on racks.

Sourdough Bread

MAKES 1 LOAF

12 oz (350 g) flour
1 tablespoon salt
8 fl oz (250 ml) Sourdough Starter
4 fl oz (120 ml) lukewarm water

1 ▲ Combine the flour and salt in a large bowl. Make a well in the centre and add the starter and water. With a wooden spoon, stir from the centre, incorporating more flour with each turn, to obtain a rough dough.

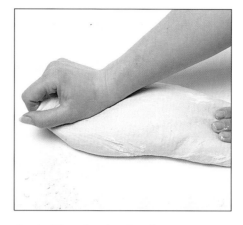

2 ▲ Transfer the dough to a floured surface. To knead, push the dough away from you with the palm of your hand, then fold it towards you, and push it away again. Repeat the process until the dough has become smooth and elastic.

3 Place in a clean bowl, cover, and leave to rise in a warm place until doubled in volume, for about 2 hours.

4 Lightly grease an 8 x 4 in (20 x 10 cm) bread tin.

5 ▼ Punch down the dough with your fist. Knead briefly, then form into a loaf shape and place in the tin, seam-side down. Cover with a plastic bag, and leave to rise in a warm place, for about 1½ hours.

6 Preheat the oven to 425°F/220°C/ Gas 7. Dust the top of the loaf with flour, then score lengthways. Bake for 15 minutes. Lower the heat to 375°F/190°C/Gas 5 and bake for about 30 minutes more, or until the bottom sounds hollow when tapped.

Sourdough Starter

MAKES 1¼ PINTS (750 ML)

1 teaspoon active dried yeast
6 fl oz (175 ml) lukewarm water
2 oz (50 g) flour ˙

~ COOK'S TIP ~

After using, feed the starter with a handful of flour and enough water to restore it to a thick batter. The starter can be refrigerated for up to 1 week, but must be brought back to room temperature before using.

1 ▲ For the starter, combine the yeast and water, stir and leave for 15 minutes to dissolve.

2 ▼ Sprinkle over the flour and whisk until it forms a batter. Cover and leave to rise in a warm place for at least 24 hours or preferably 2–4 days, before using.

Sourdough French Loaves

MAKES 2 LOAVES

2 teaspoons active dried yeast
12 fl oz (350 ml) lukewarm water
8 fl oz (250 ml) Sourdough Starter
1 lb 8 oz (700 g) plain flour
1 tablespoon salt
1 teaspoon sugar
cornmeal, for sprinkling
1 teaspoon cornflour
4 fl oz (125 ml) water

1 In a large bowl, combine the yeast and lukewarm water, stir and leave for 15 minutes to dissolve.

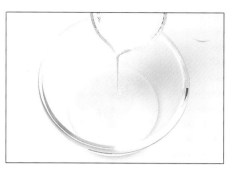

2 ▲ Pour in the sourdough starter. Add 1 lb (450 g) of the flour, the salt and the sugar. Stir until smooth. Cover the bowl with a plastic bag and leave the dough to rise in a warm place until doubled in volume, about 1½ hours.

3 Stir in just enough flour to obtain a rough dough. Transfer to a floured surface and knead until the dough is smooth and elastic. Divide in half, then shape each half into a 14 in (35 cm) cylinder with rounded ends.

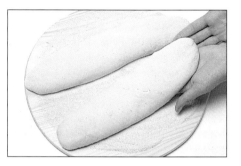

4 ▲ Place loaves on a wooden board or tray sprinkled with cornmeal. Cover loosely with a dish towel or greaseproof paper and leave to rise in a warm place until nearly doubled in volume.

5 Preheat the oven to 425°F/220°C/ Gas 7. Place a 15 x 12 in (38 x 30 cm) baking sheet in the oven. Half-fill a shallow baking dish with hot water and put it on the bottom of the oven.

6 Mix the cornflour and water in a small saucepan. Bring to the boil.

7 ▲ With a sharp knife, make several diagonal slashes across the loaves. Slide on to the hot baking sheet and brush over the cornflour mixture. Bake until the tops are golden and the bottoms sound hollow when tapped, about 25 minutes. Cool on a wire rack.

Sourdough Rye Bread

MAKES 2 LOAVES

2 teaspoons active dried yeast
4 fl oz (125 ml) lukewarm water
1 oz (30 g) butter, melted
1 tablespoon salt
4 oz (115 g) wholemeal flour
14–16 oz (400–450 g) plain flour
1 egg mixed with 1 tablespoon water, for glazing
FOR THE STARTER
1 tablespoon active dried yeast
12 fl oz (350 ml) lukewarm water
3 tablespoons black treacle
2 tablespoons caraway seeds
9 oz (250 g) rye flour

1 For the starter, combine the yeast and water, stir and leave for 15 minutes to dissolve.

2 ▲ Stir in the black treacle, caraway seeds and rye flour. Cover and leave in a warm place for 2–3 days.

3 In a large bowl, combine the yeast and water, stir and leave for 10 minutes. Stir in the melted butter, salt, wholemeal flour and 14 oz (400 g) of the plain flour.

4 ▲ Make a well in the centre and pour in the starter.

5 Stir to obtain a rough dough, then transfer to a floured surface and knead until smooth and elastic. Return to the bowl, cover and leave to rise in a warm place until doubled in volume, about 2 hours.

6 Grease a large baking sheet. Knock back the dough and knead briefly. Cut the dough in half and form each half into log-shaped loaves.

7 ▼ Place the loaves on the baking sheet and score the tops with a sharp knife. Cover and leave to rise in a warm place until almost doubled, about 50 minutes.

8 Preheat the oven to 375°F/190°C/Gas 5. Brush the loaves with the egg wash to glaze them, then bake until the bottoms sound hollow when tapped, about 50–55 minutes. If the tops brown too quickly, place a sheet of foil over the tops to protect them. Cool on a wire rack.

Wholewheat Rolls

Makes 12

2 tsp active dry yeast
2 fl oz (65 ml) lukewarm water
1 tsp caster sugar
6 fl oz (175 ml) lukewarm buttermilk
¼ tsp bicarbonate of soda
1 tsp salt
1½ oz (45 g) butter, at room temperature
7 oz (200 g) wholewheat flour
5 oz (140 g) plain flour
1 beaten egg, for glazing

1 In a large bowl, combine the yeast, water and sugar. Stir, and leave for 15 minutes to dissolve.

2 ▲ Add the buttermilk, bicarbonate of soda, salt and butter and stir to blend. Stir in the wholewheat flour.

3 Add just enough of the plain flour to obtain a rough dough.

4 Transfer to a floured surface and knead until smooth and elastic. Divide into 3 equal parts. Roll each into a cylinder, then cut in 4.

5 ▼ Form the pieces into torpedo shapes. Place on a greased baking sheet, cover and leave in a warm place until doubled in volume.

6 Preheat a 400°F/200°C/Gas 6 oven. Brush the rolls with the glaze. Bake until firm, 15–20 minutes. Cool on a rack.

French Bread

Makes 2 loaves

1 tbsp active dry yeast
16 fl oz (450 ml) lukewarm water
1 tbsp salt
1 lb 14 oz–2 lb 8 oz (850 g–1.2 kg) plain flour
semolina or flour, for sprinkling

1 Combine the yeast and water, stir, and leave for 15 minutes to dissolve. Stir in the salt.

2 Add the flour, 5 oz (140 g) at a time. Beat in with a wooden spoon, adding just enough flour to obtain a smooth dough. Alternatively, use an electric mixer with a dough hook.

3 Transfer to a floured surface and knead until smooth and elastic.

4 Shape into a ball, place in a greased bowl and cover with a plastic bag. Leave to rise in a warm place until doubled in volume, 2–4 hours.

5 ▲ Transfer to a lightly floured board and shape into 2 long loaves. Place on a baking sheet sprinkled with semolina or flour and let rise for 5 minutes.

6 ▲ Score the tops in several places with a very sharp knife. Brush with water and place in a cold oven. Set a pan of boiling water on the bottom of the oven and set the oven to 400°F/ 200°C/Gas 6. Bake until crusty and golden, about 40 minutes. Cool on a rack.

Wholewheat Rolls (top), French Bread

Pleated Rolls

MAKES 48 ROLLS

1 tablespoon active dried yeast
16 fl oz (450 ml) lukewarm milk
4 oz (115 g) margarine
5 tablespoons sugar
2 teaspoons salt
2 eggs
2 lb 3 oz–2 lb 8 oz (985 g–1.2 kg) strong flour
2 oz (55 g) butter

1 Combine the yeast and 4 fl oz (125 ml) milk in a large bowl. Stir and leave for 15 minutes to dissolve.

2 Scald the remaining milk, cool for 5 minutes, then beat in the margarine, sugar, salt and eggs. Let cool to lukewarm.

3 ▲ Pour the milk mixture into the yeast mixture. Stir in half the flour with a wooden spoon. Add the remaining flour, 5 oz (190 g) at a time, until a rough dough is obtained.

4 Transfer the dough to a lightly floured surface and knead until smooth and elastic. Place in a clean bowl, cover with a plastic bag and leave to rise in a warm place until doubled in volume, about 2 hours.

5 In a saucepan, melt the butter and set aside. Grease 2 baking sheets.

6 Punch down the dough and divide into 4 equal pieces. Roll each piece into a 12 × 8 in (30 × 20 cm) rectangle, about ¼ in (5 mm) thick.

7 ▲ Cut each of the rectangles into 4 long strips. Cut each strip into 3 4 × 2 in (10 × 5 cm) rectangles.

8 ▲ Brush each rectangle with melted butter, then fold the rectangles in half, so that the top extends about ½ in (1 cm) over the bottom.

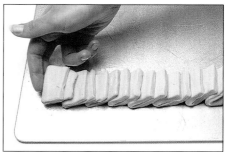

9 ▲ Place the rectangles slightly overlapping on the baking sheet, with the longer side facing up.

10 Cover and refrigerate for 30 minutes. Preheat a 350°F/180°C/Gas 4 oven. Bake until golden, 18–20 minutes. Cool slightly before serving.

Clover Leaf Rolls

MAKES 24

10 fl oz (300 ml) milk
2 tbsp caster sugar
2 oz (55 g) butter, at room temperature,
2 tsp active dry yeast
1 egg
2 tsp salt
1 lb 2 oz–1 lb 4 oz (500–575 g) plain flour
melted butter, for glazing

1 ▲ Heat the milk until lukewarm; test the temperature with your knuckle. Pour into a large bowl and stir in the sugar, butter and yeast. Leave for 15 minutes to dissolve.

2 Stir the egg and salt into the yeast mixture. Gradually stir in 1 lb 2 oz (500 g) of the flour. Add just enough extra flour to obtain a rough dough.

3 ▲ Transfer to a floured surface and knead until smooth and elastic. Place in a greased bowl, cover and leave in a warm place until doubled in volume, about 1½ hours.

4 Grease 2 12-cup bun trays.

5 ▼ Punch down the dough. Cut into 4 equal pieces. Roll each piece into a rope 14 in (35 cm) long. Cut each rope into 18 pieces, then roll each into a ball.

6 ▲ Place 3 balls, side by side, in each bun cup. Cover loosely and leave to rise in a warm place until doubled in volume, about 1½ hours.

7 Preheat a 400°F/200°C/Gas 6 oven.

8 Brush the rolls with glaze. Bake until lightly browned, about 20 minutes. Cool slightly before serving.

Poppyseed Knots

MAKES 12

10 fl oz (300 ml) lukewarm milk

2 oz (55 g) butter, at room temperature

1 tsp caster sugar

2 tsp active dry yeast

1 egg yolk

2 tsp salt

1 lb 2 oz–1 lb 4 oz (500–575 g) plain flour

1 egg beaten with 2 tsp of water, for glazing

poppyseeds, for sprinkling

1 In a large bowl, stir together the milk, butter, sugar and yeast. Leave for 15 minutes to dissolve.

2 Stir in the egg yolk, salt and 10 oz (285 g) flour. Add half the remaining flour and stir to obtain a soft dough.

3 Transfer to a floured surface and knead, adding flour if necessary, until smooth and elastic. Place in a bowl, cover and leave in a warm place until doubled in volume, 1½–2 hours.

4 ▲ Grease a baking sheet. Punch down the dough with your fist and cut into 12 pieces the size of golf balls.

5 ▲ Roll each piece to a rope, twist to form a knot and place 1 in (2.5 cm) apart on the sheet. Cover loosely and leave to rise in a warm place until doubled in volume, 1–1½ hours.

6 Preheat a 350°F/180°C/Gas 4 oven.

7 ▲ Brush the knots with the egg glaze and sprinkle over the poppyseeds. Bake until the tops are lightly browned, 25–30 minutes. Cool slightly on a rack before serving.

Bread Sticks

MAKES 18–20

1 tbsp active dry yeast
10 fl oz (300 ml) lukewarm water
15 oz (420 g) plain flour
2 tsp salt
1 tsp caster sugar
2 tbsp olive oil
5 oz (140 g) sesame seeds
1 beaten egg, for glazing
coarse salt, for sprinkling

1 Combine the yeast and water, stir and leave for 15 minutes to dissolve.

2 ▲ Place the flour, salt, sugar and olive oil in a food processor. With the motor running, slowly pour in the yeast mixture and process until the dough forms a ball. If sticky, add more flour; if dry, add more water.

3 Transfer to a floured surface and knead until smooth and elastic. Place in a bowl, cover and leave to rise in a warm place for 45 minutes.

4 ▲ Lightly toast the sesame seeds in a frying pan. Grease 2 baking sheets.

5 ▼ Roll small handfuls of dough into cylinders, about 12 in (30 cm) long. Place on the baking sheets.

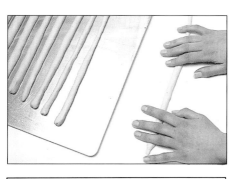

~ **VARIATION** ~

If preferred, use other seeds, such as poppy or caraway, or for plain bread sticks, omit the seeds and salt.

6 ▲ Brush with egg glaze, sprinkle with the sesame seeds, then sprinkle over some coarse salt. Leave to rise, uncovered, until almost doubled in volume, about 20 minutes.

7 Preheat a 400°F/200°C/Gas 6 oven. Bake until golden, about 15 minutes. Turn off the heat but leave the bread sticks in the oven for 5 minutes more. Serve warm or cool.

Croissants

MAKES 18

1 tbsp active dry yeast
11 fl oz (335 ml) lukewarm milk
2 tsp caster sugar
1½ tsp salt
15 oz–1 lb 2 oz (420–500 g) plain flour
8 oz (225 g) cold unsalted butter
1 egg beaten with 2 tsp water, for glazing

1 In the large bowl of an electric mixer, stir together the yeast and warm milk. Leave for 15 minutes to dissolve. Stir in the sugar, salt and 5 oz (140 g) of the flour.

2 Using a dough hook, on low speed, gradually add the remaining flour. Beat on high until the dough pulls away from the sides of the bowl. Cover and let rise in a warm place until doubled, about 1½ hours.

3 On a floured surface, knead the dough until smooth. Wrap in greaseproof paper and refrigerate for 15 minutes.

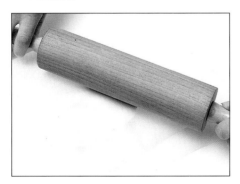

4 ▲ Divide the butter into 2 halves and place each between 2 sheets of greaseproof paper. With a rolling pin, flatten each to form a 6 × 4 in (15 × 10 cm) rectangle. Set aside.

5 ▲ On a floured surface, roll out the dough to 12 × 8 in (30 × 20 cm). Place a butter rectangle in the centre. Fold the bottom third of dough over the butter and press gently to seal. Top with the other butter rectangle, then fold over the top dough third.

6 ▲ Turn the dough so that the short side is facing you, with the long folded edge on the left and the long open edge on the right, like a book.

7 Roll the dough gently into a 12 × 8 in (30 × 20 cm) rectangle; do not press the butter out. Fold in thirds again and mark one corner with your fingertip to indicate the first turn. Wrap and refrigerate for 30 minutes.

8 Repeat twice more: again position the dough like a book, roll, fold in thirds, mark, wrap, and chill. After the third fold, refrigerate at least 2 hours (or overnight).

9 Roll out the dough about ⅛ in (3 mm) thick to a rectangle about 13 in (33 cm) wide. Trim the sides to neaten.

10 ▲ Cut the dough in half lengthwise, then cut into triangles 6 in (15 cm) high with a 4 in (10 cm) base.

11 ▲ Gently go over the triangles lengthwise with a rolling pin to stretch slightly. Roll up from base to point. Place point-down on baking sheets and curve to form a crescent. Cover and let rise in a warm place until more than doubled in volume, 1–1½ hours. (Or, refrigerate overnight and bake the next day.)

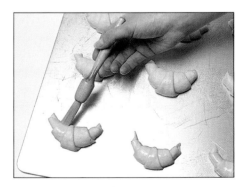

12 ▲ Preheat a 475°F/240°C/Gas 9 oven. Brush with the glaze. Bake for 2 minutes. Lower the heat to 375°F/190°C/Gas 5 and bake until golden, 10–12 more minutes. Serve warm.

Dill Bread

MAKES 2 LOAVES

4 teaspoons active dried yeast

16 fl oz (450 ml) lukewarm water

2 tablespoons sugar

2 lb 5½ oz (1.05 kg) strong flour

½ onion, chopped

4 tablespoons oil

l large bunch of dill, finely chopped

2 eggs, lightly beaten

5½ oz (150 g) cottage cheese

4 teaspoons salt

milk, for glazing

1 Mix together the yeast, water and sugar in a large bowl and leave for 15 minutes to dissolve.

2 ▼ Stir in about half of the flour. Cover and leave to rise in a warm place for 45 minutes.

3 ▲ In a frying pan, cook the onion in 1 tablespoon of the oil until soft. Set aside to cool, then stir into the yeast mixture. Stir the dill, eggs, cottage cheese, salt and remaining oil into the yeast. Gradually add the remaining flour until too stiff to stir.

4 ▲ Transfer to a floured surface and knead until smooth and elastic. Place in a bowl, cover and leave to rise until doubled in volume, 1–1½ hours.

5 ▲ Grease a large baking sheet. Cut the dough in half and shape into 2 rounds. Leave to rise in a warm place for 30 minutes.

6 Preheat a 375°F/190°C/Gas 5 oven. Score the tops, brush with the milk and bake until browned, about 50 minutes. Cool on a rack.

Spiral Herb Bread

MAKES 2 LOAVES

2 tablespoons active dried yeast
1 pt (600 ml) lukewarm water
15 oz (420 g) strong flour
1 lb 2 oz (505 g) wholemeal flour
3 teaspoons salt
1 oz (30 g) butter
1 large bunch of parsley, finely chopped
1 bunch of spring onions, chopped
1 garlic clove, finely chopped
salt and freshly ground black pepper
1 egg, lightly beaten
milk, for glazing

1 Combine the yeast and 2 fl oz (65 ml) of the water, stir and leave for 15 minutes to dissolve.

2 Combine the flours and salt in a large bowl. Make a well in the centre and pour in the yeast mixture and the remaining water. With a wooden spoon, stir from the centre, working outwards to obtain a rough dough.

3 Transfer the dough to a floured surface and knead until smooth and elastic. Return to the bowl, cover with a plastic bag, and leave until doubled in volume, about 2 hours.

4 ▲ Meanwhile, combine the butter, parsley, spring onions and garlic in a large frying pan. Cook over low heat, stirring, until softened. Season and set aside.

5 Grease 2 9 × 5 in (23 × 13 cm) tins. When the dough has risen, cut in half and roll each half into a rectangle about 14 × 9 in (35 × 23 cm).

6 ▼ Brush both with the beaten egg. Divide the herb mixture between the two, spreading just up to the edges.

7 ▲ Roll up to enclose the filling and pinch the short ends to seal. Place in the tins, seam-side down. Cover, and leave in a warm place until the dough rises above the rim of the tins.

8 Preheat a 375°F/190°C/Gas 5 oven. Brush with milk and bake until the bottoms sound hollow when tapped, about 55 minutes. Cool on a rack.

Pizza

MAKES 2

1 lb 2 oz (500 g) plain flour
1 tsp salt
2 tsp active dry yeast
10 fl oz (300 ml) lukewarm water
2–4 fl oz (65–125 ml) extra-virgin olive oil
tomato sauce, grated cheese, olives and herbs, for topping

1 Combine the flour and salt in a large mixing bowl. Make a well in the centre and add the yeast, water and 2 tablespoons of the olive oil. Leave for 15 minutes to dissolve the yeast.

2 With your hands, stir until the dough just holds together. Transfer to a floured surface and knead until smooth and elastic. Avoid adding too much flour while kneading.

3 ▲ Brush the inside of a clean bowl with 1 tablespoon of the oil. Place the dough in the bowl and roll around to coat with the oil. Cover with a plastic bag and leave to rise in a warm place until more than doubled in volume, about 45 minutes.

4 Divide the dough into 2 balls. Preheat a 400°F/200°C/Gas 6 oven.

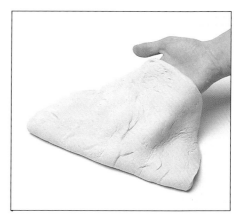

5 ▲ Roll each ball into a 10 in (25 cm) circle. Flip the circles over and onto your palm. Set each circle on the work surface and rotate, stretching the dough as you turn, until it is about 12 in (30 cm) in diameter.

6 ▲ Brush 2 pizza pans with oil. Place the dough circles in the pans and neaten the edges. Brush with oil.

7 ▲ Cover with the toppings and bake until golden, 10–12 minutes.

Cheese Bread

Makes 1 loaf

1 tablespoon active dried yeast
8 fl oz (250 ml) lukewarm milk
1 oz (30 g) butter
15 oz (420 g) strong flour
2 teaspoons salt
3½ oz (100 g) mature cheddar cheese, grated

1 Combine the yeast and milk. Stir and leave for 15 minutes to dissolve.

2 Melt the butter, let cool, and add to the yeast mixture.

3 Mix the flour and salt together in a large bowl. Make a well in the centre and pour in the yeast mixture.

4 With a wooden spoon, stir from the centre, incorporating flour with each turn, to obtain a rough dough. If the dough seems too dry, add 2–3 tablespoons water.

5 Transfer to a floured surface and knead until smooth and elastic. Return to the bowl, cover and leave to rise in a warm place until doubled in volume, 2–3 hours.

6 ▲ Grease a 9 × 5 in (23 × 13 cm) bread tin. Punch down the dough with your fist. Knead in the cheese, distributing it as evenly as possible.

7 ▼ Twist the dough, form into a loaf shape and place in the tin, tucking the ends under. Leave in a warm place until the dough rises above the rim of the tin.

8 ▲ Preheat a 400°F/200°C/Gas 6 oven. Bake for 15 minutes, then lower to 375°F/190°C/Gas 5 and bake until the bottom sounds hollow when tapped, about 30 minutes more.

Italian Flat Bread With Sage

MAKES 1 LOAF

2 teaspoons active dried yeast
8 fl oz (250 ml) lukewarm water
12 oz (375 g) plain flour
2 teaspoons salt
5 tablespoons extra virgin olive oil
12 fresh sage leaves, chopped

1   Combine the yeast and water, stir and leave for 15 minutes until the yeast has completely dissolved.

2   Mix the flour and salt in a large bowl, and make a well in the centre.

3   Stir in the yeast mixture and 4 tablespoons of the oil. Stir from the centre, incorporating flour with each turn, to obtain a rough dough.

4   ▲ Transfer the dough to a lightly floured surface and knead until it is smooth and elastic. Shape into a ball and place in a lightly oiled bowl. Cover and leave to rise in a warm place until doubled in volume, for about 2 hours.

5   Preheat the oven to 400°F/200°C/ Gas 6 and place a baking sheet in the centre of the oven.

6   Punch down the dough. Knead in the sage leaves, then roll into a 12 in (30 cm) round. Leave to rise slightly.

7   ▼ Dimple the surface all over with your finger. Drizzle the remaining oil on top. Slide a floured board under the bread, carry to the oven, and slide off on the hot baking sheet. Bake for about 35 minutes, or until golden brown. Cool on a rack.

Courgette Yeast Bread

SERVES 10

1 lb (450 g) courgettes, grated
2 tablespoons salt
2 teaspoons active dried yeast
½ pint (300 ml) lukewarm water
14 oz (400 g) plain flour
olive oil, for brushing

1   In a colander, alternate the layers of grated courgettes and salt. Leave for 30 minutes, then squeeze out the moisture with your hands.

2   Combine the yeast with 2 fl oz (50 ml) warm water. Leave for 15 minutes.

3   ▲ Place the courgettes, yeast and flour in a bowl. Stir together and add just enough of the remaining water to obtain a rough dough.

4   Transfer to a floured surface and knead until smooth and elastic. Return the dough to the bowl, cover with a plastic bag, and leave to rise in a warm place until doubled in volume, for about 1½ hours.

5   Punch down the risen dough with your fist and knead into a tapered cylinder. Place on a greased baking sheet, cover and leave to rise in a warm place until doubled in volume.

6   ▼ Preheat the oven to 425°F/ 220°C/Gas 7. Brush the bread with olive oil and bake for 40–45 minutes, or until the loaf is a golden colour.

Italian Flat Bread with Sage (top), Courgette Yeast Bread

Olive Bread

MAKES 2 LOAVES

4 teaspoons active dried yeast
16 fl oz (450 ml) warm water
14 oz (400 g) plain flour
6 oz (170 g) wholemeal flour
2½ oz (70 g) cornmeal
2 teaspoons salt
2 tablespoons olive oil
4 oz (115 g) mixed stoned green and black olives, cut in half
cornmeal, for sprinkling

1 Combine the yeast and water, stir and leave for 5 minutes to dissolve.

2 Stir in 8 oz (225 g) of the plain flour, cover and leave in a warm place for 1 hour.

3 In a large mixing bowl, combine the remaining plain flour, the wholemeal flour, cornmeal and salt. Make a well in the centre; pour in the olive oil and yeast mixture.

4 ▼ With a wooden spoon, stir from the centre, incorporating flour with each turn. When the dough becomes stiff, stir with your hands until a rough dough is obtained.

5 Transfer to a floured surface and knead until smooth and elastic. Return to the bowl, cover and leave to rise in a warm place until doubled in volume, about 1½ hours.

6 ▲ Knock back the dough with your fist. Add the olives and knead.

7 Cut the dough in half and shape each half into a round. Sprinkle a baking sheet with cornmeal. Place the rounds on the sheet, seam-side down. Cover and leave to rise until nearly doubled in volume.

8 Place a baking tin in the bottom of the oven and half fill it with hot water. Preheat the oven to 425°F/220°C/Gas 7.

9 ▲ With a sharp knife, score the tops of the loaves. Bake for 20 minutes. Lower the heat to 375°F/190°C/Gas 5 and bake for 25–30 minutes more, or until the bottoms sound hollow when tapped. Cool on a wire rack.

Pumpkin Spice Bread

Makes 1 Loaf

2 tablespoons active dried yeast
8 fl oz (250 ml) lukewarm water
2 teaspoons ground cinnamon
1 teaspoon ground ginger
1 teaspoon ground allspice
¼ teaspoon ground cloves
1 teaspoon salt
3 oz (85 g) dried skimmed milk
6 oz (170 g) cooked or canned pumpkin
12 oz (350 g) sugar
4 oz (115 g) butter, melted
1 lb 6 oz (625 g) plain flour
2 oz (55 g) pecans, finely chopped

1 Using an electric mixer, combine the yeast and water, stir and leave for 15 minutes to dissolve. In another bowl, mix the spices together.

2 To the yeast, add the salt, milk, pumpkin, 115 g (4 oz) of the sugar, 3 tablespoons of the melted butter, 2 teaspoons of the spice mixture and 8 oz (225 g) of the flour.

3 ▲ With the dough hook, mix on low speed until blended. Gradually add the remaining flour and mix on medium speed until a rough dough is formed. Alternatively, mix by hand.

4 Transfer to a floured surface and knead until smooth. Place in a bowl, cover and leave to rise in a warm place until doubled, 1–1½ hours.

5 ▼ Knock back and knead briefly. Divide the dough into thirds. Roll each third into an 18 in (46 cm) rope. Cut each rope into 18 equal pieces, then roll into balls.

6 Grease a 10 in (25 cm) tube tin. Stir the remaining sugar into the remaining spice mixture. Roll the balls in the remaining melted butter, then in the sugar and spice mixture.

7 ▲ Place 18 balls in the tin and sprinkle over half the pecans. Add the remaining balls, then sprinkle over the remaining pecans. Cover and leave to rise in a warm place until almost doubled, about 45 minutes.

8 Preheat the oven to 350°F/180°C/ Gas 4. Bake for 55 minutes. Cool in the tin for 20 minutes, then turn out on a rack. Serve warm.

Walnut Bread

MAKES 1 LOAF

15 oz (420 g) wholemeal flour

5 oz (140 g) strong flour

2½ teaspoons salt

18 fl oz (525 ml) lukewarm water

1 tablespoon honey

1 tablespoon active dried yeast

5 oz (140 g) walnut pieces, plus more for decorating

1 beaten egg, for glazing

1 Combine the flours and salt in a large bowl. Make a well in the centre and add 8 fl oz (250 ml) of the water, the honey and the yeast.

2 Set aside until the yeast dissolves and the mixture is frothy.

3 Add the remaining water. With a wooden spoon, stir from the centre, incorporating flour with each turn, to obtain a smooth dough. Add more flour if the dough is too sticky and use your hands if the dough becomes too stiff to stir.

4 Transfer to a floured board and knead, adding flour if necessary, until the dough is smooth and elastic. Place in a greased bowl and roll the dough around in the bowl to coat thoroughly on all sides.

5 ▲ Cover with a plastic bag and leave in a warm place until doubled in volume, about 1½ hours.

6 ▲ Punch down the dough and knead in the walnuts evenly.

7 Grease a baking sheet. Shape into a round loaf and place on the baking sheet. Press in walnut pieces to decorate the top. Cover loosely with a damp cloth and leave to rise in a warm place until doubled, 25–30 minutes.

8 Preheat a 425°F/220°C/Gas 7 oven.

9 ▲ With a sharp knife, score the top. Brush with the glaze. Bake for 15 minutes. Lower the heat to 375°F/190°C/Gas 5 and bake until the bottom sounds hollow when tapped, about 40 minutes. Cool on a rack.

Pecan Rye Bread

MAKES 2 LOAVES

1½ tablespoons active dried yeast
24 fl oz (700 ml) lukewarm water
1 lb 8 oz (700 g) strong flour
1 lb 2 oz (500 g) rye flour
2 tablespoons salt
1 tablespoon honey
2 teaspoons caraway seeds, (optional)
4 oz (115 g) butter, at room temperature
8 oz (225 g) pecans, chopped

1 Combine the yeast and 4 fl oz (125 ml) of the water. Stir and leave for 15 minutes to dissolve.

2 In the bowl of an electric mixer, combine the flours, salt, honey, caraway seeds and butter. With the dough hook, mix on low speed until well blended.

3 Add the yeast mixture and the remaining water and mix on medium speed until the dough forms a ball.

4 ▲ Transfer to a floured surface and knead in the pecans.

5 Return the dough to a bowl, cover with a plastic bag and leave in a warm place until doubled, about 2 hours.

6 Grease 2 8½ × 4½ in (21.5 × 11.5 cm) bread tins.

7 ▲ Punch down the risen dough.

8 Divide the dough in half and form into loaves. Place in the tins, seam-side down. Dust the tops with flour.

9 Cover with plastic bags and leave to rise in a warm place until doubled in volume, about 1 hour.

10 Preheat a 375°F/190°C/Gas 5 oven.

11 ▼ Bake until the bottoms sound hollow when tapped, 45–50 minutes. Cool on racks.

Sticky Buns

MAKES 18

5½ fl oz (170 ml) milk
1 tablespoon active dried yeast
2 tablespoons caster sugar
15 oz–1 lb (420–450 g) strong flour
1 teaspoon salt
4 oz (115 g) cold butter, cut into pieces
2 eggs, lightly beaten
grated rind of 1 lemon

FOR THE TOPPING AND FILLING

10 oz (285 g) dark brown sugar
2½ oz (70 g) butter
4 fl oz (125 ml) water
3 oz (85 g) pecans or walnuts, chopped
3 tablespoons caster sugar
2 teaspoons ground cinnamon
5½ oz (150 g) raisins

1 Heat the milk to lukewarm. Add the yeast and sugar and leave until frothy, about 15 minutes.

2 Combine the flour and salt in a large mixing bowl. Add the butter and rub in with your fingertips until the mixture resembles coarse breadcrumbs.

3 ▲ Make a well in the centre and add the yeast mixture, eggs and lemon rind. With a wooden spoon, stir from the centre, incorporating flour with each turn. When it becomes too stiff, stir by hand to obtain a rough dough.

4 Transfer to a floured surface and knead until smooth and elastic. Return to the bowl, cover with a plastic bag and leave to rise in a warm place until doubled in volume, about 2 hours.

5 Meanwhile, for the topping, make the syrup. Combine the brown sugar, butter and water in a heavy saucepan. Bring to the boil and boil gently until thick and syrupy, about 10 minutes.

6 ▲ Place 1 tablespoon of the syrup in the bottom of each of 18 1½ in (4 cm) muffin cups. Sprinkle in a thin layer of chopped nuts, reserving the rest for the filling.

7 Punch down the dough and transfer to a floured surface. Roll out to an 18 × 12 in (45 × 30 cm) rectangle.

8 ▲ For the filling, combine the caster sugar, cinnamon, raisins and reserved nuts. Sprinkle over the dough in an even layer.

9 ▲ Roll up tightly, from the long side, to form a cylinder.

10 ▲ Cut the cylinder into 1 in (2.5 cm) rounds. Place each in a prepared muffin cup, cut-side up. Leave to rise in a warm place until increased by half, about 30 minutes.

11 Preheat a 350°F/180°C/Gas 4 oven. Place foil under the tins to catch any syrup that bubbles over. Bake until golden, about 25 minutes.

12 Remove from the oven and invert the tins onto a baking sheet. Leave for 3–5 minutes, then remove buns from the tins. Transfer to a rack to cool. Serve sticky-side up.

~ COOK'S TIP ~

To save time and energy, make double the recipe and freeze half for another occasion.

Raisin Bread

MAKES 2 LOAVES

1 tablespoon active dried yeast
16 fl oz (450 ml) lukewarm milk
5 oz (140 g) raisins
2½ oz (70 g) currants
1 tablespoon sherry or brandy
½ teaspoon grated nutmeg
grated rind of 1 large orange
2¼ oz (60 g) sugar
1 tablespoon salt
4 oz (115 g) butter, melted
1 lb 8 oz–1 lb 14 oz (700–850 g) strong flour
1 egg beaten with 1 tablespoon cream, for glazing

1 Stir together the yeast and 4 fl oz (125 ml) of the milk and let stand for 15 minutes to dissolve.

2 ▲ Mix the raisins, currants, sherry or brandy, nutmeg and orange rind together and set aside.

3 In another bowl, mix the remaining milk, sugar, salt and half the butter. Add the yeast mixture. With a wooden spoon, stir in half the flour, 5 oz (140 g) at a time, until blended. Add the remaining flour as needed for a stiff dough.

4 Transfer to a floured surface and knead until smooth and elastic. Place in a greased bowl, cover and leave to rise in a warm place until doubled in volume, about 2½ hours.

5 Punch down the dough, return to the bowl, cover and leave to rise in a warm place for 30 minutes.

6 Grease 2 8½ × 4½ in (21.5 × 11.5 cm) bread tins. Divide the dough in half and roll each half into a 20 × 7 in (50 × 18 cm) rectangle.

7 ▲ Brush the rectangles with the remaining melted butter. Sprinkle over the raisin mixture, then roll up tightly, tucking in the ends slightly as you roll. Place in the prepared tins, cover, and leave to rise until almost doubled in volume.

8 ▲ Preheat a 400°F/200°C/Gas 6 oven. Brush the loaves with the glaze. Bake for 20 minutes. Lower to 350°F/180°C/Gas 4 and bake until golden, 25–30 minutes more. Cool on racks.

Prune Bread

MAKES 1 LOAF

8 oz (225 g) dried prunes
1 tablespoon active dried yeast
3 oz (85 g) wholemeal flour
13½–15 oz (385–420 g) strong flour
½ teaspoon bicarbonate of soda
1 teaspoon salt
1 teaspoon pepper
1 oz (30 g) butter, at room temperature
6 fl oz (175 ml) buttermilk
2 oz (55 g) walnuts, chopped
milk, for glazing

1 Simmer the prunes in water to cover until soft, or soak overnight. Drain, reserving 2 fl oz (65 ml) of the soaking liquid. Stone and chop the prunes.

2 Combine the yeast and the reserved prune liquid, stir and leave for 15 minutes to dissolve.

3 In a large bowl, stir together the flours, bicarbonate of soda, salt and pepper. Make a well in the centre.

4 ▲ Add the chopped prunes, butter, and buttermilk. Pour in the yeast mixture. With a wooden spoon, stir from the centre, incorporating more flour with each turn, to obtain a rough dough.

5 Transfer to a floured surface and knead until smooth and elastic. Return to the bowl, cover with a plastic bag and leave to rise in a warm place until doubled in volume, about 1½ hours.

6 Grease a baking sheet.

7 ▲ Punch down the dough with your fist, then knead in the walnuts.

8 Shape the dough into a long, cylindrical loaf. Place on the baking sheet, cover loosely, and leave to rise in a warm place for 45 minutes.

9 Preheat a 425°F/220°C/Gas 7 oven.

10 ▼ With a sharp knife, score the top deeply. Brush with milk and bake for 15 minutes. Lower to 375°F/190°C/Gas 5 and bake until the bottom sounds hollow when tapped, about 35 minutes more. Cool.

Plaited Prune Bread

MAKES 1 LOAF

1 tbsp active dry yeast
2 fl oz (65 ml) lukewarm water
2 fl oz (65 ml) lukewarm milk
2 oz (55 g) caster sugar
½ tsp salt
1 egg
2 oz (55 g) butter, at room temperature
15 oz–1 lb 2 oz (420–500 g) plain flour
1 egg beaten with 2 tsp water, for glazing
FOR THE FILLING
7 oz (200 g) cooked prunes
2 tsp grated lemon rind
1 tsp grated orange rind
¼ tsp freshly grated nutmeg
1½ oz (45 g) butter, melted
2 oz (55 g) very finely chopped walnuts
2 tbsp caster sugar

1 In a large bowl, combine the yeast and water, stir and leave for 15 minutes to dissolve.

2 Stir in the milk, sugar, salt, egg and butter. Gradually stir in 12 oz (350 g) of the flour to obtain a soft dough.

3 Transfer to a floured surface and knead in just enough flour to obtain a dough that is smooth and elastic. Put into a clean bowl, cover and leave to rise in a warm place until doubled in volume, about 1½ hours.

~ VARIATION ~

For Plaited Apricot Bread, replace the prunes with the same amount of dried apricots. It is not necessary to cook them, but to soften, soak them in hot tea and discard the liquid before using.

4 ▲ Meanwhile, for the filling, combine the prunes, lemon and orange rinds, nutmeg, butter, walnuts and sugar and stir together to blend. Set aside.

5 Grease a large baking sheet. Punch down the dough and transfer to a lightly floured surface. Knead briefly, then roll out into a 15 × 10 in (38 × 25 cm) rectangle. Carefully transfer to the baking sheet.

6 ▲ Spread the filling in the centre.

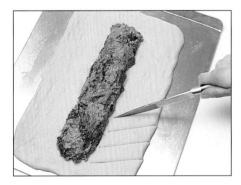

7 ▲ With a sharp knife, cut 10 strips at an angle on either side of the filling, cutting just to the filling.

8 ▲ For a plaited pattern, fold up one end neatly, then fold over the strips from alternating sides until all the strips are folded over. Tuck excess dough underneath at the ends.

9 ▲ Cover loosely with a tea towel and leave to rise in a warm place until almost doubled in volume.

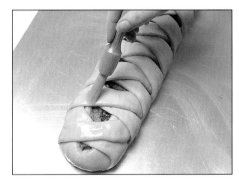

10 ▲ Preheat a 375°F/190°C/Gas 5 oven. Brush with the glaze. Bake until browned, about 30 minutes. Transfer to a rack to cool.

Kugelhopf

MAKES 1 LOAF

3¾ oz (110 g) raisins

1 tablespoon kirsch or brandy

1 tablespoon active dried yeast

4 fl oz (125 ml) lukewarm water

4 oz (115 g) unsalted butter, at room temperature

3½ oz (100 g) sugar

3 eggs, at room temperature

grated rind of 1 lemon

1 teaspoon salt

½ teaspoon vanilla essence

15 oz (420 g) strong flour

4 fl oz (125 ml) milk

1 oz (30 g) flaked almonds

3¼ oz (90 g) whole blanched almonds, chopped

icing sugar, for dusting

1 ▼ In a bowl, combine the raisins and kirsch or brandy. Set aside.

2 Combine the yeast and water, stir and leave for 15 minutes to dissolve.

3 With an electric mixer, cream the butter and sugar until thick and fluffy. Beat in the eggs, one at a time. Add the lemon rind, salt and vanilla. Stir in the yeast mixture.

4 ▲ Add the flour, alternating with the milk, until the mixture is well blended. Cover and leave to rise in a warm place until doubled in volume, about 2 hours.

5 ▲ Grease a 4½ pt kugelhopf mould, then sprinkle the flaked almonds evenly over the bottom.

6 Work the raisins and almonds into the dough, then spoon into the mould. Cover with a plastic bag, and leave to rise in a warm place until the dough almost reaches the top of the tin, about 1 hour.

7 Preheat a 350°F/180°C/Gas 4 oven.

8 Bake until golden brown, about 45 minutes. If the top browns too quickly, protect with a sheet of foil. Let cool in the tin for 15 minutes, then turn out onto a rack. Dust the top lightly with icing sugar before serving.

Panettone

MAKES 1 LOAF

5 fl oz (150 ml) lukewarm milk
1 tablespoon active dried yeast
12–14 oz (350–400 g) plain flour
2½ oz (70 g) sugar
2 teaspoons salt
2 eggs
5 egg yolks
6 oz (170 g) unsalted butter, at room temperature
4½ oz (125 g) raisins
grated rind of 1 lemon
3 oz (85 g) mixed peel

1 Combine the milk and yeast in a large warmed bowl and leave for 10 minutes to dissolve.

2 Stir in 4 oz (115 g) of the flour, cover loosely and leave in a warm place for 30 minutes.

3 Sift over the remaining flour and stir into the dough mixture. Make a well in the centre and add the sugar, salt, eggs and egg yolks.

4 ▲ Stir with a wooden spoon until stiff, then stir with your hands to obtain a very elastic and sticky dough. Add a little more flour if necessary, but keep the dough as soft as possible.

5 ▲ To incorporate the butter, smear it over the dough, then work it in with your hands. When the butter is evenly distributed, cover and leave to rise in a warm place until doubled in volume, 3–4 hours.

6 Grease a 3½ pint (2 litre) charlotte tin or a 2 lb 4 oz (1 kg) coffee tin and line the bottom with greaseproof paper. Grease the paper.

7 Knock back the dough and transfer to a floured surface. Knead in the raisins, lemon rind and mixed peel.

8 ▲ Put the dough in the tin. Cover and leave to rise in a warm place until it is well above the top of the tin, about 2 hours.

9 Preheat the oven to 400°F/200°C/Gas 6. Bake for 15 minutes, cover the top with foil and lower the heat to 350°F/180°C/Gas 4. Bake for 30 minutes more. Cool in the tin for 5 minutes, then transfer to a rack.

Danish Wreath

SERVES 10–12

¼ oz (7 g) active dried yeast
6 fl oz (175 ml) lukewarm milk
2 oz (55 g) caster sugar
1 lb (450 g) strong flour
½ teaspoon salt
½ teaspoon vanilla essence
1 egg, beaten
2 × 4 oz (115 g) blocks unsalted butter
1 egg yolk beaten with 2 teaspoons water, for glazing
4 oz (115 g) icing sugar
1–2 tablespoons water
chopped pecans or walnuts, for sprinkling

FOR THE FILLING

7 oz (200 g) dark brown sugar
1 teaspoon ground cinnamon
2 oz (55 g) pecans or walnuts, toasted and chopped

1 Combine the yeast, milk and ½ teaspoon of the sugar. Stir and leave for 15 minutes to dissolve.

2 Combine the flour, sugar and salt. Make a well in the centre and add the yeast mixture, vanilla and egg. Stir until a rough dough is formed.

3 Transfer to a floured surface and knead until smooth and elastic. Wrap and refrigerate for 15 minutes.

> ### ~ VARIATION ~
>
> For a different filling, substitute 3 tart apples, peeled and grated, the grated rind of 1 lemon, 1 tablespoon lemon juice, ½ teaspoon ground cinnamon, 3 tablespoons sugar, 1¼ oz (35 g) currants, and 1 oz (30 g) chopped walnuts. Combine well and use as described.

4 ▲ Meanwhile, place the butter between two sheets of greaseproof paper. With a rolling pin, flatten to form 2 6 × 4 in (15 × 10 cm) rectangles. Set aside.

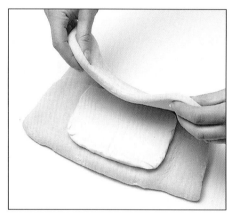

5 ▲ Roll out the dough to a 12 × 8 in (30 × 20 cm) rectangle. Place one butter rectangle in the centre. Fold the bottom third of dough over the butter and seal the edge. Place the other butter rectangle on top and cover with the top third of the dough.

6 Turn the dough so the shorter side faces you. Roll into an 12 × 8 in (30 × 20 cm) rectangle. Fold into thirds, and indent one edge with your finger to indicate the first turn. Wrap in clear film and refrigerate for 30 minutes.

7 Repeat two more times; rolling, folding, marking and chilling between each turn. After the third fold refrigerate for 1–2 hours, or longer.

8 Grease a large baking sheet. In a bowl, stir together all the filling ingredients until blended.

9 ▲ Roll out the dough to a 25 × 6 in (3 × 15 cm) strip. Spread over the filling, leaving a ½ in (1 cm) border.

10 Roll up the dough lengthways into a cylinder. Place on the baking sheet and form into a circle, pinching the edges together to seal. Cover with an inverted bowl and leave in a warm place to rise for 45 minutes.

11 ▲ Preheat the oven to 400°F/200°C/Gas 6. Slash the top every 2 in (5 cm), cutting about ½ in (1 cm) deep. Brush with the egg glaze. Bake until golden, 35–40 minutes. Cool on a rack. To serve, mix the icing sugar and water, then drizzle over the wreath. Sprinkle with the pecans or walnuts.

PIES & TARTS

~

Here is every sort of filling – from orchard fruits to autumn nuts, tangy citrus to luscious chocolate – for the most memorable pies and tarts. Some are plain and some are fancy, but all are delicious.

Plum Pie

SERVES 8

2 lb (900 g) red or purple plums

grated rind of 1 lemon

1 tbsp fresh lemon juice

4–6 oz (115–170 g) caster sugar

3 tbsp quick-cooking tapioca

⅛ tsp salt

½ tsp ground cinnamon

¼ tsp grated nutmeg

FOR THE PASTRY

10 oz (285 g) plain flour

1 tsp salt

3 oz (85 g) cold butter, cut in pieces

2 oz (55 g) cold vegetable fat or lard, cut in pieces

2–4 fl oz (65–125 ml) iced water

milk, for glazing

1 ▼ For the pastry, sift the flour and salt into a bowl. Add the butter and fat and cut in with a pastry blender until the mixture resembles coarse breadcrumbs.

2 Stir in just enough water to bind the pastry. Gather into 2 balls, 1 slightly larger than the other. Wrap and refrigerate for 20 minutes.

3 Preheat a baking sheet in the centre of a 425°F/220°C/Gas 7 oven.

4 On a lightly floured surface, roll out the larger pastry ball to about ⅛ in (3 mm) thick. Transfer to a 9 in (23 cm) pie dish and trim the edge.

5 ▲ Halve the plums, discard the stones, and cut in large pieces. Mix all the filling ingredients together (if the plums are very tart, use extra sugar). Transfer to the pastry case.

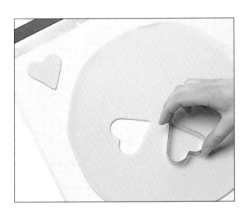

6 ▲ Roll out the remaining pastry and place on a baking tray lined with greaseproof paper. With a cutter, stamp out 4 hearts. Transfer the pastry lid to the pie using the paper.

7 Trim to leave a ¾ in (2 cm) overhang. Fold the top edge under the bottom and pinch to seal. Arrange the hearts on top. Brush with the milk. Bake for 15 minutes. Reduce the heat to 350°F/180°C/Gas 4 and bake 30–35 minutes more. If the crust browns too quickly, protect with a sheet of foil.

Lattice Berry Pie

SERVES 8

1 lb (450 g) berries, such as bilberries, blueberries, blackcurrants etc
4 oz (115 g) caster sugar
3 tbsp cornflour
2 tbsp fresh lemon juice
1 oz (30 g) butter, diced
FOR THE PASTRY
10 oz (285 g) plain flour
¾ tsp salt
4 oz (115 g) cold butter, cut in pieces
1½ oz (45 g) cold vegetable fat or lard, cut in pieces
5–6 tbsp iced water
1 egg beaten with 1 tbsp water, for glazing

1 For the pastry, sift the flour and salt into a bowl. Add the butter and fat and cut in with a pastry blender until the mixture resembles coarse breadcrumbs. With a fork, stir in just enough water to bind the pastry. Form into 2 balls, wrap in greaseproof paper, and refrigerate for 20 minutes.

2 On a lightly floured surface, roll out one ball about ⅛ in (3 mm) thick. Transfer to a 9 in (23 cm) pie dish and trim to leave a ½ in (1 cm) overhang. Brush the bottom with egg glaze.

3 ▲ Mix all the filling ingredients together, except the butter (reserve a few berries for decoration). Spoon into the pastry case and dot with the butter. Brush the egg glaze around the rim of the pastry case.

4 Preheat a baking sheet in the centre of a 425°F/220°C/Gas 7 oven.

5 ▼ Roll out the remaining pastry on a baking tray lined with greaseproof paper. With a serrated pastry wheel, cut out 24 thin pastry strips. Roll out the scraps and cut out leaf shapes. Mark veins in the leaves with the point of a knife.

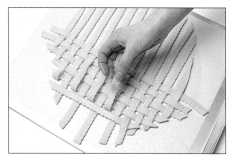

6 ▲ Weave the strips in a close lattice, then transfer to the pie using the paper. Press the edges to seal and trim. Arrange the pastry leaves around the rim. Brush with egg glaze.

7 Bake for 10 minutes. Reduce the heat to 350°F/180°C/Gas 4 and bake until the pastry is golden, 40–45 minutes more. Decorate with berries.

Raspberry Tart

SERVES 8

4 egg yolks
2½ oz (70 g) caster sugar
3 tbsp plain flour
10 fl oz (300 ml) milk
⅛ tsp salt
½ tsp vanilla essence
1 lb (450 g) fresh raspberries
5 tbsp red currant jelly
1 tbsp fresh orange juice
FOR THE PASTRY
6½ oz (190 g) plain flour
½ tsp baking powder
¼ tsp salt
1 tbsp sugar
grated rind of ½ orange
3 oz (85 g) cold butter, cut in pieces
1 egg yolk
3–4 tbsp whipping cream

1 For the pastry, sift the flour, baking powder and salt into a bowl. Stir in the sugar and orange rind. Add the butter and cut in with a pastry blender until the mixture resembles coarse breadcrumbs. Stir in the egg yolk and just enough cream to bind the dough. Gather into a ball, wrap in greaseproof paper and refrigerate.

2 For the custard filling, beat the egg yolks and sugar until thick and lemon-coloured. Gradually stir in the flour.

3 In a saucepan, bring the milk and salt just to the boil, then remove from the heat. Whisk into the egg yolk mixture, return to the pan and continue whisking over moderately high heat until just bubbling. Cook for 3 minutes to thicken. Transfer immediately to a bowl. Add the vanilla and stir to blend.

4 ▲ Cover with greaseproof paper to prevent a skin from forming.

5 ▲ Preheat a 400°F/200°C/Gas 6 oven. On a floured surface, roll out the pastry ⅛ in (3 mm) thick, transfer to a 10 in (25 cm) pie dish and trim. Prick the bottom with a fork and line with crumpled greaseproof. Fill with baking beans and bake for 15 minutes. Remove the paper and beans. Continue baking until golden, 6–8 minutes more. Let cool.

6 ▲ Spread an even layer of the pastry cream filling in the pastry case and arrange the raspberries on top. Melt the jelly and orange juice in a pan and brush on top to glaze.

Rhubarb and Cherry Pie

SERVES 8

1 lb (450 g) rhubarb, cut into 1 in (2.5 cm) pieces
1 lb (450 g) canned stoned tart red or black cherries, drained
10 oz (285 g) caster sugar
1 oz (30 g) quick-cooking tapioca
FOR THE PASTRY
10 oz (285 g) plain flour
1 tsp salt
3 oz (85 g) cold butter, cut in pieces
2 oz (55 g) cold vegetable fat or lard, cut in pieces
2–4 fl oz (65–125 ml) iced water
milk, for glazing

1 ▲ For the pastry, sift the flour and salt into a bowl. Add the butter and fat to the dry ingredients and cut in with a pastry blender until the mixture resembles coarse breadcrumbs.

2 With a fork, stir in just enough water to bind the pastry. Gather into 2 balls, 1 slightly larger than the other. Wrap the pastry in greaseproof paper and refrigerate for at least 20 minutes.

3 Preheat a baking sheet in the centre of a 400°F/200°C/Gas 6 oven.

4 On a lightly floured surface, roll out the larger pastry ball to a thickness of about ⅛ in (3 mm).

5 ▼ Roll the pastry around the rolling pin and transfer to a 9 in (23 cm) pie dish. Trim the edge to leave a ½ in (1 cm) overhang.

6 Refrigerate the pastry case while making the filling.

7 In a mixing bowl, combine the rhubarb, cherries, sugar and tapioca and spoon into the pie shell.

8 ▲ Roll out the remaining pastry and cut out leaf shapes.

9 Transfer the pastry lid to the pie and trim to leave a ¾ in (2 cm) overhang. Fold the top edge under the bottom and flute. Roll small balls from the scraps. Mark veins in the pastry leaves and place on top with the balls.

10 Glaze the top and bake until golden, 40–50 minutes.

Peach Leaf Pie

SERVES 8

2 lb 8 oz (1.2 kg) ripe peaches

juice of 1 lemon

3½ oz (100 g) sugar

3 tablespoons cornflour

¼ teaspoon grated nutmeg

½ teaspoon ground cinnamon

1 oz (30 g) butter, diced

FOR THE CRUST

10 oz (285 g) plain flour

¾ teaspoon salt

4 oz (115 g) cold butter, cut into
    pieces

2¼ oz (60 g) cold vegetable fat or lard,
    cut into pieces

5–6 tablespoons iced water

1 egg beaten with 1 tablespoon water,
    for glazing

1 For the pastry, sift the flour and salt into a bowl. Add the butter and fat and rub in with your fingertips until the mixture resembles coarse breadcrumbs.

2 ▲ With a fork, stir in just enough water to bind the dough. Gather into 2 balls, one slightly larger than the other. Wrap in clear film and refrigerate for at least 20 minutes.

3 Place a baking sheet in the oven and preheat to 425°F/220°C/Gas 7.

4 ▲ Drop a few peaches at a time into boiling water for 20 seconds, then transfer to a bowl of cold water. When cool, peel off the skins.

5 Slice the peaches and combine with the lemon juice, sugar, cornstarch and spices. Set aside.

6 ▲ On a lightly floured surface, roll out the larger dough ball about ⅛ in (3 mm) thick. Transfer to a 9 in (23 cm) pie tin and trim. Refrigerate.

7 ▲ Roll out the remaining dough ¼ in (5 mm) thick. Cut out leaf shapes 3 in (8 cm) long, using a template if needed. Mark veins with a knife. With the scraps, roll a few balls.

8 ▲ Brush the bottom of the pastry shell with egg glaze. Add the peaches, piling them higher in the centre. Dot with the butter.

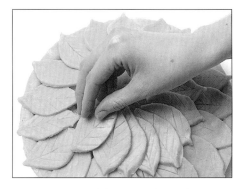

9 ▲ To assemble, start from the outside edge and cover the peaches with a ring of leaves. Place a second ring of leaves above, staggering the positions. Continue with rows of leaves until covered. Place the balls in the centre. Brush with glaze.

10 Bake for 10 minutes. Lower the heat to 350°F/180°C/Gas 4 and bake for 35–40 minutes more.

~ COOK'S TIP ~

Baking the pie on a preheated baking sheet helps to make the bottom crust crisp. The moisture from the filling keeps the bottom crust more humid than the top, but this baking method helps to compensate for the top crust being better exposed to the heat source.

Peach Tart with Almond Cream

SERVES 8–10

4 large ripe peaches
4 oz (115 g) blanched almonds
2 tbsp plain flour
3½ oz (100 g) unsalted butter, at room temperature
4 oz (115 g) plus 2 tbsp caster sugar
1 egg
1 egg yolk
½ tsp vanilla essence, or 2 tsp rum
FOR THE PASTRY
6½ oz (190 g) plain flour
¾ tsp salt
3½ oz (100 g) cold unsalted butter, cut in pieces
1 egg yolk
2½–3 tbsp iced water

1 ▲ For the pastry, sift the flour and salt into a bowl.

2 Add the butter and cut in with a pastry blender until the mixture resembles coarse breadcrumbs. Stir in the egg yolk and just enough water to bind the pastry. Gather into a ball, wrap in greaseproof paper, and refrigerate for at least 20 minutes.

3 Preheat a baking sheet in the centre of a 400°F/200°C/Gas 6 oven.

4 ▲ On a floured surface, roll out the pastry ⅛ in (3 mm) thick. Transfer to a 10 in (25 cm) pie dish. Trim the edge, prick the bottom and refrigerate.

5 ▲ Score the bottoms of the peaches. Drop the peaches, 1 at a time, into boiling water. Boil for 20 seconds, then dip in cold water. Peel off the skins using a sharp knife.

6 ▲ Grind the almonds finely with the flour in a food processor, blender or grinder. With an electric mixer, cream the butter and 4 oz (115 g) of the sugar until light and fluffy. Gradually beat in the egg and yolk. Stir in the almonds and vanilla or rum. Spread in the pastry case.

7 ▲ Halve the peaches and remove the stones. Cut crosswise in thin slices and arrange on top of the almond cream like the spokes of a wheel; keep the slices of each peach-half together. Fan out by pressing down gently at a slight angle.

8 ▲ Bake until the pastry begins to brown, 10–15 minutes. Lower the heat to 350°F/180°C/Gas 4 and continue baking until the almond cream sets, about 15 minutes more. Ten minutes before the end of the cooking time, sprinkle with the remaining 2 tablespoons of sugar.

~ **VARIATION** ~

For a Nectarine and Apricot Tart with Almond Cream, replace the peaches with nectarines, prepared and arranged the same way. Peel and chop 3 fresh apricots. Fill the spaces between the fanned-out nectarines with 1 tablespoon of chopped apricots. Bake as above.

Apple and Cranberry Lattice Pie

SERVES 8

grated rind of 1 orange

3 tablespoons fresh orange juice

2 large, tart cooking apples

6 oz (170 g) cranberries

2½ oz (70 g) raisins

1 oz (30 g) walnuts, chopped

7½ oz (215 g) caster sugar

4 oz (115 g) dark brown sugar

2 tablespoons plain flour

FOR THE CRUST

10 oz (285 g) plain flour

½ teaspoon salt

3 oz (85 g) cold butter, cut into pieces

3 oz (85 g) cold vegetable fat or lard, cut
   into pieces

2–4 fl oz (65–125 ml) iced water

1 ▼ For the crust, sift the flour and salt into a bowl. Add the butter and fat and rub in with your fingertips until the mixture resembles coarse breadcrumbs. With a fork, stir in just enough water to bind the dough. Gather into 2 equal balls, wrap in cling film, and refrigerate for at least 20 minutes.

2 ▲ Put the orange rind and juice into a mixing bowl. Peel and core the apples and grate into the bowl. Stir in the cranberries, raisins, walnuts, all except 1 tablespoon of the caster sugar, the brown sugar and flour.

3 Place a baking sheet in the oven and preheat to 400°F/200°C/Gas 6.

4 On a lightly floured surface, roll out 1 ball of dough about ⅛ in (3 mm) thick. Transfer to a 9 in (23 cm) pie plate and trim. Spoon the cranberry and apple mixture into the shell.

5 ▲ Roll out the remaining dough to a circle about 11 in (28 cm) in diameter. With a serrated pastry wheel, cut the dough into 10 strips, ¾ in (2 cm) wide. Place 5 strips horizontally across the top of the tart at 1 in (2.5 cm) intervals. Weave in 5 vertical strips and trim. Sprinkle the top with the remaining sugar.

6 Bake for 20 minutes. Reduce the heat to 350°F/180°C/Gas 4 and bake until the crust is golden and the filling is bubbling, about 15 minutes more.

Open Apple Pie

SERVES 8

3 lb (1.4 kg) sweet-tart firm eating or cooking apples
1¾ oz (50 g) sugar
2 teaspoons ground cinnamon
grated rind and juice of 1 lemon
1 oz (30 g) butter, diced
2–3 tablespoons honey
FOR THE CRUST
10 oz (285 g) plain flour
½ teaspoon salt
4 oz (115 g) cold butter, cut into pieces
2¼ oz (60 g) cold vegetable fat or lard, cut into pieces
5–6 tablespoons iced water

1 For the crust, sift the flour and salt into a bowl. Add the butter and fat and rub in with your fingertips until the mixture resembles coarse breadcrumbs.

2 ▲ With a fork, stir in just enough water to bind the dough. Gather into a ball, wrap in clear film, and refrigerate for at least 20 minutes.

3 Place a baking sheet in the centre of the oven and preheat to 400°F/200°C/Gas 6.

4 ▼ Peel, core, and slice the apples. Combine the sugar and cinnamon in a bowl. Add the apples, lemon rind and juice and stir.

5 On a lightly floured surface, roll out the dough to a circle about 12 in (30 cm) in diameter. Transfer to a 9 in (23 cm) diameter deep pie dish; leave the dough hanging over the edge. Fill with the apple slices.

6 ▲ Fold in the edges and crimp loosely for a decorative border. Dot the apples with diced butter.

7 Bake on the hot sheet until the pastry is golden and the apples are tender, about 45 minutes.

8 Melt the honey in a saucepan and brush over the apples to glaze. Serve warm or at room temperature.

Apple Pie

SERVES 8

2 lb (900 g) tart cooking apples
2 tbsp plain flour
4 oz (115 g) caster sugar
1½ tbsp fresh lemon juice
½ tsp ground cinnamon
½ tsp ground allspice
¼ tsp ground ginger
¼ tsp grated nutmeg
¼ tsp salt
2 oz (55 g) butter, diced
FOR THE PASTRY
10 oz (285 g) plain flour
1 tsp salt
3 oz (85 g) cold butter, cut in pieces
2 oz (55 g) cold vegetable fat or lard, cut in pieces
2–4 fl oz (65–125 ml) iced water

1 ▲ For the crust, sift the flour and salt into a bowl.

2 Add the butter and fat and cut in with a pastry blender or rub between your fingertips until the mixture resembles coarse breadcrumbs. With a fork, stir in just enough water to bind the pastry.

3 ▲ Form 2 balls, wrap in greaseproof paper and refrigerate for 20 minutes.

4 ▲ On a lightly floured surface, roll out 1 ball ⅛ in (3 mm) thick. Transfer to a 9 in (23 cm) pie dish and trim the edge. Preheat a baking sheet in the centre of a 425°F/220°C/Gas 7 oven.

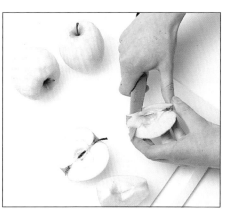

5 ▲ Peel, core and slice the apples into a bowl. Toss with the flour, sugar, lemon juice, spices and salt. Spoon into pie shell; dot with butter.

6 ▲ Roll out the remaining pastry. Place on top of the pie and trim to leave a ¾ in (2 cm) overhang. Fold the overhang under the pastry base and press to seal. Crimp the edge.

7 ▲ Roll out the scraps and cut out leaf shapes and roll balls. Arrange on top of the pie. Cut steam vents.

8 Bake for 10 minutes. Reduce the heat to 350°F/180°C/Gas 4 and bake until golden, 40–45 minutes more. If the pie browns too quickly, protect with foil.

~ **COOK'S TIP** ~

Instead of using cooking apples, choose crisp eaters such as Granny Smith, that will not soften too much during cooking.

Pear and Apple Crumble Pie

SERVES 8

3 firm pears

4 cooking apples

6 oz (170 g) caster sugar

2 tbsp cornflour

⅛ tsp salt

grated rind of 1 lemon

2 tbsp fresh lemon juice

3 oz (85 g) raisins

3 oz (85 g) plain flour

1 tsp ground cinnamon

3 oz (85 g) cold butter, cut in pieces

FOR THE PASTRY

5 oz (140 g) plain flour

½ tsp salt

2½ oz (70 g) cold vegetable fat or lard, cut in pieces

2 tbsp iced water

1 For the pastry, combine the flour and salt in a bowl. Add the fat and cut in with a pastry blender until the mixture resembles coarse breadcrumbs. Stir in just enough water to bind the pastry. Gather into a ball and transfer to a lightly floured surface. Roll out ⅛ in (3 mm) thick.

2 ▲ Transfer to a shallow 9 in (23 cm) pie dish and trim to leave a ½ in (1 cm) overhang. Fold the overhang under for double thickness. Flute the edge. Refrigerate.

3 Preheat a baking sheet in the centre of a 450°F/230°C/Gas 8 oven.

4 ▲ Peel and core the pears. Slice them into a bowl. Peel, core and slice the apples. Add to the pears. Stir in one-third of the sugar, the cornflour, salt and lemon rind. Add the lemon juice and raisins and stir to blend.

5 For the crumble topping, combine the remaining sugar, flour, cinnamon, and butter in a bowl. Blend with your fingertips until the mixture resembles coarse breadcrumbs. Set aside.

6 ▲ Spoon the fruit filling into the pastry case. Sprinkle the crumbs lightly and evenly over the top.

7 Bake for 10 minutes, then reduce the heat to 350°F/180°C/Gas 4. Cover the top of the pie loosely with a sheet of foil and continue baking until browned, 35–40 minutes more.

Chocolate Pear Tart

SERVES 8

4 oz (115 g) plain chocolate, grated
3 large firm, ripe pears
1 egg
1 egg yolk
4 fl oz (125 ml) single cream
½ tsp vanilla essence
3 tbsp caster sugar
FOR THE PASTRY
5 oz (140 g) plain flour
⅛ tsp salt
2 tbsp sugar
4 oz (115 g) cold unsalted butter, cut into pieces
1 egg yolk
1 tbsp fresh lemon juice

1 For the pastry, sift the flour and salt into a bowl. Add the sugar and butter. Cut in with a pastry blender until the mixture resembles coarse breadcrumbs. Stir in the egg yolk and lemon juice until the mixture forms a ball. Wrap in greaseproof paper, and refrigerate for at least 20 minutes.

2 Preheat a baking sheet in the centre of a 400°F/200°C/Gas 6 oven.

3 On a lightly floured surface, roll out the pastry ⅛ in (3 mm) thick. Transfer to a 10 in (25 cm) tart dish and trim.

4 ▲ Sprinkle the bottom of the case with the grated chocolate.

5 ▲ Peel, halve and core the pears. Cut in thin slices crosswise, then fan them out slightly.

6 Transfer the pear halves to the tart with the help of a metal spatula and arrange on top of the chocolate like the spokes of a wheel.

7 ▼ Whisk together the egg and egg yolk, cream and vanilla. Ladle over the pears, then sprinkle with sugar.

8 Bake for 10 minutes. Reduce the heat to 350°F/180°C/Gas 4 and cook until the custard is set and the pears begin to caramelize, about 20 minutes more. Serve warm.

Caramelized Upside-Down Pear Pie

SERVES 8

5–6 firm, ripe pears
6 oz (170 g) sugar
4 oz (115 g) unsalted butter
whipped cream, for serving
FOR THE PASTRY
4 oz (115 g) plain flour
¼ teaspoon salt
4½ oz (125 g) cold butter, cut into pieces
1½ oz (45 g) cold vegetable fat, cut into pieces
4 tablespoons iced water

1 ▲ For the pastry, combine the flour and salt in a bowl. Add the butter and vegetable fat and cut in with a pastry blender until the mixture resembles coarse crumbs. With a fork, stir in enough iced water to bind the dough. Gather into a ball, wrap in clear film and refrigerate for at least 20 minutes. Preheat the oven to 400°F/200°C/Gas 6.

> ~ **VARIATION** ~
>
> For Caramelized Upside-Down Apple Pie, replace the pears with 8–9 firm, tart apples. There may seem to be too many apples, but they shrink slightly as they cook.

2 ▲ Quarter, peel and core the pears. Place in a bowl and toss with a few tablespoons of the sugar.

3 ▲ In a 10½ in (27 cm) ovenproof frying pan, melt the butter over moderately high heat. Add the remaining sugar. When it starts to colour, arrange the pears evenly around the edge and in the centre.

4 ▲ Continue cooking, uncovered, until caramelized, about 20 minutes.

5 ▲ Let the fruit cool. Roll out a circle of dough slightly larger than the diameter of the pan. Place the dough on top of the pears, tucking it around the edges. Transfer the pan to the oven and bake for 15 minutes, then reduce the heat to 350°F/180°C/Gas 4. Bake until golden, about 15 minutes more.

6 ▲ Let the pie cool in the pan for about 3–4 minutes. Run a knife around the edge of the pan to loosen the pie, ensuring that the knife reaches down to the bottom of the pan. Invert a plate on top and, protecting your hands with oven gloves, hold plate and pan firmly, and turn them both over quickly.

7 Lift off the pan. If any pears stick to the pan, remove them gently with a metal spatula and replace them carefully on the pie. Serve warm, with the whipped cream passed separately.

Lime Tart

Serves 8

3 large egg yolks

1 × 14 oz (400 g) can sweetened
  condensed milk

1 tbsp grated lime rind

4 fl oz (125 ml) fresh lime juice

green food colouring (optional)

4 fl oz (125 ml) whipping cream

For the base

4 oz (115 g) digestive biscuits, crushed

2½ oz (70 g) butter or margarine, melted

1 Preheat a 350°F/180°C/Gas 4 oven.

2 ▲ For the base, place the crushed biscuits in a bowl and add the butter or margarine. Mix to combine.

> ~ **VARIATION** ~
>
> Use lemons instead of limes,
> with yellow food colouring.

3 Press the mixture evenly over the bottom and sides of a 9 in (23 cm) pie dish. Bake for 8 minutes. Let cool.

4 ▲ Beat the yolks until thick. Beat in the milk, lime rind and juice and colouring, if using. Pour into the pastry case and refrigerate until set, about 4 hours. To serve, whip the cream. Pipe a lattice pattern on top, or spoon dollops around the edge.

Fruit Tartlets

Makes 8

6 fl oz (175 ml) red currant jelly

1 tbsp fresh lemon juice

6 fl oz (175 ml) whipping cream

1½ lb (700 g) fresh fruit, such as strawberries, raspberries, kiwi fruit, peaches, grapes or currants, peeled and sliced as necessary

For the pastry

5 oz (140 g) cold butter, cut in pieces

2½ oz (65 g) dark brown sugar

3 tbsp cocoa powder

7 oz (200 g) plain flour

1 egg white

1 For the pastry, combine the butter, brown sugar and cocoa over low heat. When the butter is melted, remove from the heat and sift over the flour. Stir, then add just enough egg white to bind the mixture. Gather into a ball, wrap in greaseproof paper, and refrigerate for 30 minutes.

2 ▲ Grease 8 3 in (8 cm) tartlet tins. Roll out the pastry between 2 sheets of greaseproof paper. Stamp out 8 4 in (10 cm) rounds with a fluted cutter.

3 Line the tartlet tins. Prick the bottoms. Refrigerate for 15 minutes. Preheat a 350°F/180°C/Gas 4 oven.

4 Bake until firm, 20–25 minutes. Cool, then remove from the tins.

5 ▲ Melt the jelly with the lemon juice. Brush a thin layer in the bottom of the tartlets. Whip the cream and spread a thin layer in the tartlet cases. Arrange the fruit on top. Brush with the glaze and serve.

Lime Tart (top), Fruit Tartlets

Chocolate Lemon Tart

SERVES 8–10

8¾ oz (240 g) caster sugar

6 eggs

grated rind of 2 lemons

5½ fl oz (170 ml) fresh lemon juice

5½ fl oz (170 ml) whipping cream

chocolate curls, for decorating

FOR THE CRUST

6¼ oz (180 g) plain flour

2 tablespoons unsweetened cocoa powder

1 oz (30 g) icing sugar

½ teaspoon salt

4 oz (115 g) butter or margarine

1 tablespoon water

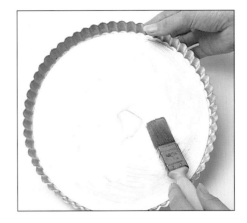

1 ▲ Grease a 10 in (25 cm) tart tin.

2 For the crust, sift the flour, cocoa powder, icing sugar and salt into a bowl. Set aside.

3 ▲ Melt the butter and water over a low heat. Pour over the flour mixture and stir with a wooden spoon until the dough is smooth and the flour has absorbed all the liquid.

4 Press the dough evenly over the base and side of the prepared tart tin. Refrigerate the tart shell while preparing the filling.

5 Preheat a baking sheet in a 375°F/ 190°C/Gas 5 oven.

6 ▲ Whisk the sugar and eggs until the sugar is dissolved. Add the lemon rind and juice and mix well. Add the cream. Taste the mixture and add more lemon juice or sugar if needed. It should taste tart but also sweet.

7 Pour the filling into the tart shell and bake on the hot sheet until the filling is set, 20–25 minutes. Cool on a rack. When cool, decorate with the chocolate curls.

Lemon Almond Tart

SERVES 8

5½ oz (150 g) whole blanched almonds

3½ oz (100 g) sugar

2 eggs

grated rind and juice of 1½ lemons

4 oz (115 g) butter, melted

strips of lemon rind, for decorating

FOR THE CRUST

6¼ oz (180 g) plain flour

1 tablespoon sugar

½ teaspoon salt

½ teaspoon baking powder

3 oz (85 g) cold unsalted butter, cut into pieces

3–4 tablespoons whipping cream

1 For the crust, sift the flour, sugar, salt and baking powder into a bowl. Add the butter and rub in with your fingertips until the mixture resembles coarse breadcrumbs.

2 ▲ With a fork, stir in just enough cream to bind the dough.

3 Gather into a ball and transfer to a lightly floured surface. Roll out the dough about ⅛ in (3 mm) thick and transfer to a 9 in (23 cm) tart tin. Trim and prick the base all over with a fork. Refrigerate for at least 20 minutes.

4 Preheat a baking sheet in a 400°F/200°C/Gas 6 oven.

5 Line the tart shell with crumpled greaseproof paper and fill with dried beans. Bake for 12 minutes. Remove the paper and beans and continue baking until golden, 6–8 minutes more. Reduce the oven temperature to 350°F/180°C/Gas 4.

6 ▲ Grind the almonds finely with 1 tablespoon of the sugar in a food processor, blender, or coffee grinder.

7 ▲ Set a mixing bowl over a pan of hot water. Add the eggs and the remaining sugar, and beat with an electric mixer until the mixture is thick enough to leave a ribbon trail when the beaters are lifted.

8 Stir in the lemon rind and juice, butter and ground almonds.

9 Pour into the prebaked shell. Bake until the filling is golden and set, about 35 minutes. Decorate with lemon rind.

Lemon Meringue Pie

SERVES 8

| grated rind and juice of 1 large lemon |
| 8 fl oz (250 ml) plus 1 tbsp cold water |
| 4 oz (115 g) plus 6 tbsp caster sugar |
| 1 oz (30 g) butter |
| 3 tbsp cornflour |
| 3 eggs, separated |
| ⅛ tsp salt |
| ⅛ tsp cream of tartar |
| FOR THE PASTRY |
| 5 oz (140 g) plain flour |
| ½ tsp salt |
| 2½ oz (70 g) cold vegetable fat or lard, cut in pieces |
| 2 tbsp iced water |

1 For the pastry, sift the flour and salt into a bowl. Add the fat and cut in with a pastry blender until the mixture resembles coarse breadcrumbs. With a fork, stir in just enough water to bind the mixture. Gather the pastry into a ball.

2 ▲ On a lightly floured surface, roll out the pastry about ⅛ in (3 mm) thick. Transfer to a 9 in (23 cm) pie dish and trim the edge to leave a ½ in (2 cm) overhang.

3 ▲ Fold the overhang under and crimp the edge. Refrigerate the pastry case for at least 20 minutes.

4 Preheat a 400°F/200°C/Gas 6 oven.

5 ▲ Prick the case all over with a fork. Line with crumpled greaseproof paper and fill with baking beans. Bake for 12 minutes. Remove the paper and beans and continue baking until golden, 6–8 minutes more.

6 In a saucepan, combine the lemon rind and juice, 8 fl oz (250 ml) of the water, 4 oz (115 g) of the sugar, and butter. Bring the mixture to a boil.

7 Meanwhile, in a mixing bowl, dissolve the cornflour in the remaining water. Add the egg yolks.

~ **VARIATION** ~

For Lime Meringue Pie, substitute the grated rind and juice of 2 medium-sized limes for the lemon.

8 ▲ Add the egg yolks to the lemon mixture and return to the boil, whisking continuously until the mixture thickens, about 5 minutes.

9 Cover the surface with greaseproof paper and let cool.

10 ▲ For the meringue, using an electric mixer beat the egg whites with the salt and cream of tartar until they hold stiff peaks. Add the remaining sugar and beat until glossy.

11 ▲ Spoon the lemon mixture into the pastry case and level. Spoon the meringue on top, smoothing it up to the pastry rim to seal. Bake until golden, 12–15 minutes.

Orange Tart

SERVES 8

7 oz (200 g) sugar

8 fl oz (250 ml) fresh orange juice, strained

2 large navel oranges

5½ oz (150 g) whole blanched almonds

2 oz (55 g) butter

1 egg

1 tablespoon plain flour

3 tablespoons apricot jam

FOR THE CRUST

7½ oz (215 g) plain flour

½ teaspoon salt

2 oz (55 g) cold butter, cut into pieces

1½ oz (45 g) cold margarine, cut into pieces

3–4 tablespoons iced water

1 For the crust, sift the flour and salt into a bowl. Add the butter and margarine and rub in with your fingertips until the mixture resembles coarse breadcrumbs. Stir in just enough water to bind the dough. Gather into a ball, wrap in clear film, and refrigerate for at least 20 minutes.

2 On a lightly floured surface, roll out the dough ¼ in (5 mm) thick and transfer to an 8 in (20 cm) tart tin. Trim off the overhang. Refrigerate until needed.

3 In a saucepan, combine 5½ oz (150 g) of the sugar and the orange juice and boil until thick and syrupy, about 10 minutes.

4 ▲ Cut the oranges into ¼ in (5 mm) slices. Do not peel. Add to the syrup. Simmer gently for 10 minutes, or until glazed. Transfer to a rack to dry. When cool, cut in half. Reserve the syrup. Place a baking sheet in the oven and heat to 400°F/200°C/Gas 6.

5 Grind the almonds finely in a food processor, blender or coffee grinder. With an electric mixer, cream the butter and remaining sugar until light and fluffy. Beat in the egg and 2 tablespoons of the orange syrup. Stir in the almonds and flour.

6 Melt the jam over low heat, then brush over the tart shell. Pour in the almond mixture. Bake until set, about 20 minutes. Let cool.

7 ▲ Arrange overlapping orange slices on top. Boil the remaining syrup until thick. Brush on top to glaze.

Pumpkin Pie

SERVES 8

1 lb (450 g) cooked or canned pumpkin
8 fl oz (250 ml) whipping cream
2 eggs
4 oz (115 g) dark brown sugar
4 tablespoons golden syrup
1½ teaspoons ground cinnamon
1 teaspoon ground ginger
¼ teaspoon ground cloves
½ teaspoon salt
FOR THE PASTRY
6 oz (170 g) plain flour
½ teaspoon salt
3 oz (85 g) cold butter, cut into pieces
1½ oz (45 g) cold vegetable fat, cut into pieces
3–4 tablespoons iced water

1 For the pastry, sift the flour and salt into a bowl. Cut in the butter and fat until it resembles coarse crumbs. Bind with iced water. Wrap in clear film and refrigerate for 20 minutes.

2 Roll out the dough and line a 9 in (23 cm) pie tin. Trim off the overhang. Roll out the trimmings and cut out leaf shapes. Wet the rim of the pastry case with a brush dipped in water.

3 ▲ Place the dough leaves around the rim. Chill for 20 minutes. Preheat the oven to 400°F/200°C/Gas 6.

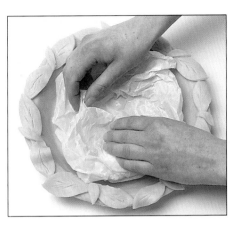

4 ▲ Line the pastry case with greaseproof paper. Fill with baking beans and bake for 12 minutes. Remove paper and beans and bake until golden, 6–8 minutes more. Reduce the heat to 375°F/ 190°C/Gas 5.

5 ▼ Beat together the pumpkin, cream, eggs, sugar, golden syrup, spices and salt. Pour into the pastry case and bake until set, 40 minutes.

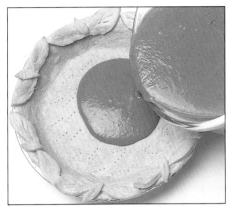

Maple Walnut Tart

SERVES 8

3 eggs

⅛ tsp salt

2 oz (55 g) caster sugar

2 oz (55 g) butter or margarine, melted

8 fl oz (250 ml) pure maple syrup

4 oz (115 g) chopped walnuts

whipped cream, for decorating

FOR THE PASTRY

2½ oz (70 g) plain flour

2½ oz (70 g) wholewheat flour

⅛ tsp salt

2 oz (55 g) cold butter, cut in pieces

1½ oz (45 g) cold vegetable fat or lard, cut in pieces

1 egg yolk

2–3 tbsp iced water

1 ▼ For the pastry, mix the flours and salt in a bowl. Add the butter and fat and cut in with a pastry blender until the mixture resembles coarse breadcrumbs. With a fork, stir in the egg yolk and just enough water to bind the pastry. Form into a ball.

2 Wrap in greaseproof paper and refrigerate for 20 minutes.

3 Preheat a 425°F/220°C/Gas 7 oven.

4 On a lightly floured surface, roll out the pastry about ⅛ in (3 mm) thick and transfer to a 9 in (23 cm) pie dish. Trim the edge. To decorate, roll out the trimmings. With a small heart-shaped cutter, stamp out enough hearts to go around the rim of the pie. Brush the edge with water, then arrange the pastry hearts all around.

5 ▲ Prick the bottom with a fork. Line with crumpled greaseproof paper and fill with baking beans. Bake for 10 minutes. Remove the paper and beans and continue baking until golden brown, 3–6 minutes more.

6 In a bowl, whisk the eggs, salt and sugar together. Stir in the butter and maple syrup.

7 ▲ Set the pastry case on a baking sheet. Pour in the filling, then sprinkle the nuts over the top.

8 Bake until just set, about 35 minutes. Cool on a rack. Decorate with whipped cream, if wished.

Pecan Tart

SERVES 8

3 eggs

⅛ tsp salt

7 oz (200 g) dark brown sugar

4 fl oz (125 ml) golden syrup

2 tbsp fresh lemon juice

3 oz (85 g) butter, melted

5 oz (140 g) chopped pecan nuts

2 oz (55 g) pecan halves

FOR THE PASTRY

6 oz (170 g) plain flour

1 tbsp caster sugar

1 tsp baking powder

½ tsp salt

3 oz (85 g) cold unsalted butter, cut in pieces

1 egg yolk

3–4 tbsp whipping cream

1 For the pastry, sift the flour, sugar, baking powder and salt into a bowl. Add the butter and cut in with a pastry blender until the mixture resembles coarse breadcrumbs.

2 ▼ In a bowl, beat together the egg yolk and cream until blended.

~ **COOK'S TIP** ~

Serve this tart warm, accompanied by ice cream or whipped cream, if wished.

3 ▲ Pour the cream mixture into the flour mixture and stir with a fork.

4 Gather the pastry into a ball. On a lightly floured surface, roll out ⅛ in (3 mm) thick and transfer to a 9 in (23 cm) pie dish. Trim the overhang and flute the edge with your fingers. Refrigerate for at least 20 minutes.

5 Preheat a baking sheet in the middle of a 400°F/200°C/Gas 6 oven.

6 In a bowl, lightly whisk the eggs and salt. Add the sugar, syrup, lemon juice and butter. Mix well and stir in the chopped nuts.

7 ▲ Pour into the pastry case and arrange the pecan halves in concentric circles on top.

8 Bake for 10 minutes. Reduce the heat to 325°F/170°C/Gas 3; continue baking 25 minutes more.

Mince Pies

MAKES 36

6 oz (170 g) finely chopped blanched almonds

5 oz (140 g) dried apricots, finely chopped

6 oz (170 g) raisins

5 oz (140 g) currants

5 oz (140 g) glacé cherries, chopped

5 oz (140 g) cut mixed peel, chopped

4 oz (115 g) finely chopped beef suet

grated rind and juice of 2 lemons

grated rind and juice of 1 orange

7 oz (200 g) dark brown sugar

4 cooking apples, peeled, cored and chopped

2 tsp ground cinnamon

1 tsp grated nutmeg

½ tsp ground cloves

8 fl oz (250 ml) brandy

8 oz (225 g) cream cheese

2 tbsp caster sugar

icing sugar, for dusting (optional)

FOR THE PASTRY

15 oz (420 g) plain flour

5 oz (140 g) icing sugar

12 oz (350 g) cold butter, cut in pieces

grated rind and juice of 1 orange

milk, for glazing

1 Mix the nuts, dried and preserved fruit, suet, citrus rind and juice, brown sugar, apples and spices.

2 ▲ Stir in the brandy. Cover and leave in a cool place for 2 days.

3 For the pastry, sift the flour and icing sugar into a bowl. Cut in the butter until the mixture resembles coarse breadcrumbs.

4 ▲ Add the orange rind. Stir in just enough orange juice to bind. Gather into a ball, wrap in greaseproof paper, and refrigerate for at least 20 minutes.

5 Preheat a 425°F/220°C/Gas 7 oven. Grease 2–3 bun trays. Beat together the cream cheese and sugar.

6 ▲ Roll out the pastry ¼ in (5 mm) thick. With a fluted pastry cutter, stamp out 36 3 in (8 cm) rounds.

~ COOK'S TIP ~

The mincemeat mixture may be packed into sterilized jars and sealed. It will keep refrigerated for several months. Add a few tablespoonfuls to give apple pies a lift, or make small mincemeat-filled parcels using filo pastry.

7 ▲ Transfer the rounds to the bun tray. Fill halfway with mincemeat. Top with a teaspoonful of the cream cheese mixture.

8 ▲ Roll out the remaining pastry and stamp out 36 2 in (5 cm) rounds with a fluted cutter. Brush the edges of the pies with milk, then set the rounds on top. Cut a small steam vent in the top of each pie.

9 ▲ Brush lightly with milk. Bake until golden, 15–20 minutes. Let cool for 10 minutes before unmoulding. Dust with icing sugar, if wished.

Shoofly Pie

SERVES 8

4 oz (115 g) plain flour
4 oz (115 g) dark brown sugar
¼ teaspoon each salt, ground ginger, cinnamon, mace and grated nutmeg
3 oz (85 g) cold butter, cut into pieces
2 eggs
4 fl oz (125 ml) molasses
4 fl oz (125 ml) boiling water
½ teaspoon bicarbonate of soda
FOR THE PASTRY
4 oz (115 g) cream cheese, at room temperature, cut into pieces
4 oz (115 g) cold butter, at room temperature, cut into pieces
4 oz (115 g) plain flour

1 For the pastry, put the cream cheese and butter in a mixing bowl. Sift over the flour.

2 ▲ Cut in with a pastry blender until the dough just holds together. Wrap in clear film and refrigerate for at least 30 minutes.

3 Put a baking sheet in the centre of the oven and preheat the oven to 375°F/190°C/Gas 5.

4 In a bowl, mix the flour, sugar, salt and spices. Rub in the butter with your fingertips until the mixture resembles coarse crumbs. Set aside.

5 On a lightly floured surface, roll out the dough and line a 9 in (23 cm) pie tin. Trim the overhanging pastry and flute the rim.

6 ▲ Spoon a third of the crumbed mixture into the pastry case.

7 ▲ To complete the filling, whisk the eggs with the molasses in a large bowl until combined.

8 Pour the boiling water into a small bowl. Stir in the bicarbonate of soda; the mixture will foam. Immediately whisk into the egg mixture. Pour carefully into the pastry case and sprinkle the remaining crumbed mixture evenly over the top.

9 Stand on the hot baking sheet and bake until browned, about 35 minutes. Leave to cool to room temperature, then serve.

Treacle Tart

SERVES 4–6

6 fl oz (175 ml) golden syrup

3 oz (85 g) fresh white breadcrumbs

grated rind of 1 lemon

2 tbsp fresh lemon juice

FOR THE PASTRY

6 oz (170 g) plain flour

½ tsp salt

3 oz (85 g) cold butter, cut in pieces

1½ oz (45 g) cold margarine, cut in pieces

3–4 tbsp iced water

1 For the pastry, combine the flour and salt in a bowl. Add the butter and margarine and cut in with a pastry blender until the mixture resembles coarse breadcrumbs.

2 ▲ With a fork, stir in just enough water to bind the pastry. Gather into a ball, wrap in greaseproof paper, and refrigerate for at least 20 minutes.

3 On a lightly floured surface, roll out the pastry ⅛ in (3 mm) thick. Transfer to an 8 in (20 cm) pie dish and trim off the overhang. Refrigerate for at least 20 minutes. Reserve the trimmings for the lattice top.

4 Preheat a baking sheet at the top of a 400°F/200°C/Gas 6 oven.

5 In a saucepan, warm the syrup until thin and runny.

6 ▲ Remove from the heat and stir in the breadcrumbs and lemon rind. Let sit for 10 minutes so the bread can absorb the syrup. Add more breadcrumbs if the mixture is thin. Stir in the lemon juice and spread evenly in the pastry case.

7 Roll out the pastry trimmings and cut into 10–12 thin strips.

8 ▼ Lay half the strips on the filling, then lay the remaining strips at an angle over them to form a lattice.

9 Place on the hot sheet and bake for 10 minutes. Lower the heat to 375°F/190°C/Gas 5. Bake until golden, about 15 minutes more. Serve warm or cold.

Chess Pie

SERVES 8

2 eggs
3 tablespoons whipping cream
4 oz (115 g) dark brown sugar
2 tablespoons granulated sugar
2 tablespoons plain flour
1 tablespoon whisky
1½ oz (45 g) butter, melted
2 oz (55 g) chopped walnuts
3 oz (85 g) stoned dates
whipped cream, for serving
FOR THE PASTRY
3 oz (85 g) cold butter
1½ oz (45 g) cold vegetable fat
6 oz (170 g) plain flour
½ teaspoon salt
3–4 tablespoons iced water

1 ▲ For the pastry, cut the butter and fat into small pieces.

2 Sift the flour and salt into a bowl. With a pastry blender, cut in the butter and fat until the mixture resembles coarse crumbs. Stir in just enough water to bind. Gather into a ball, wrap in greaseproof paper and refrigerate for at least 20 minutes.

3 Place a baking sheet in the oven and preheat it to 375°F/190°C/Gas 5.

4 Roll out the dough thinly and line a 9 in (23 cm) pie tin. Trim the edge. Roll out the trimmings, cut thin strips and plait them. Brush the edge of the pastry case with water and fit the pastry plaits around the rim.

5 ▲ In a mixing bowl, whisk together the eggs and cream.

6 Add both sugars and beat until well combined. Sift over 1 tablespoon of the flour and stir in. Add the whisky, the melted butter and the walnuts. Stir to combine.

7 ▲ Mix the dates with the remaining tablespoon of flour and stir into the walnut mixture.

8 Pour into the pastry case and bake until the pastry is golden and the filling puffed up, about 35 minutes. Serve at room temperature, with whipped cream, if liked.

Coconut Cream Tart

SERVES 8

5 oz (140 g) desiccated coconut
5 oz (140 g) caster sugar
4 tbsp cornflour
⅛ tsp salt
1 pt (625 ml) milk
2 fl oz (65 ml) whipping cream
2 egg yolks
1 oz (30 g) unsalted butter
2 tsp vanilla essence
FOR THE PASTRY
5 oz (140 g) plain flour
¼ tsp salt
1½ oz (45 g) cold butter, cut in pieces
1 oz (30 g) cold vegetable fat or lard
2–3 tbsp iced water

1 For the pastry, sift the flour and salt into a bowl. Add the butter and fat and cut in with a pastry blender until the mixture resembles coarse breadcrumbs.

2 ▲ With a fork, stir in just enough water to bind the pastry. Gather into a ball, wrap in greaseproof paper and refrigerate for 20 minutes.

3 Preheat a 425°F/220°C/Gas 7 oven. Roll out the pastry ⅛ in (3 mm) thick. Line a 9 in (23 cm) pie dish. Trim and flute the edges. Prick the bottom. Line with crumpled greaseproof and fill with baking beans. Bake 10–12 minutes. Remove paper and beans, reduce heat to 350°F/180°C/Gas 4 and bake until brown, 10–15 minutes.

4 ▲ Spread 2 oz (55 g) of the coconut on a baking sheet and toast in the oven until golden, 6–8 minutes, stirring often. Set aside for decorating.

5 Put the sugar, cornflour and salt in a saucepan. In a bowl, whisk the milk, cream and egg yolks. Add the egg mixture to the saucepan.

6 ▼ Cook over a low heat, stirring, until the mixture comes to the boil. Boil for 1 minute, then remove from the heat. Add the butter, vanilla and remaining coconut.

7 Pour into the prebaked pastry case. When cool, sprinkle toasted coconut in a ring in the centre.

Black Bottom Pie

SERVES 8

2 teaspoons gelatin

3 tablespoons cold water

2 eggs, separated

5 oz (140 g) caster sugar

½ oz (15 g) cornflour

½ teaspoon salt

16 fl oz (450 ml) milk

2 oz (55 g) plain chocolate, finely
    chopped

2 tablespoons rum

¼ teaspoon cream of tartar

chocolate curls, for decorating

FOR THE CRUST

6 oz (170 g) gingersnaps, crushed

2½ oz (70 g) butter, melted

1 Preheat a 350°F/180°C/Gas 4 oven.

2 For the crust, mix the crushed
gingersnaps and melted butter.

3 ▲ Press the mixture evenly over
the bottom and side of a 9 in (23 cm)
pie plate. Bake for 6 minutes.

4 Sprinkle the gelatin over the water
and let stand to soften.

5 Beat the egg yolks in a large mixing
bowl and set aside.

6 In a saucepan, combine half the
sugar, the cornflour and salt.
Gradually stir in the milk. Boil for 1
minute, stirring constantly.

7 ▲ Whisk the hot milk mixture
into the yolks, then pour all back into
the saucepan and return to the boil,
whisking. Cook for 1 minute, still
whisking. Remove from the heat.

8 ▲ Measure out 8 oz (225 g) of the
hot custard mixture and pour into a
bowl. Add the chopped chocolate to
the custard mixture, and stir until
melted. Stir in half the rum and pour
into the pie shell.

9 ▲ Whisk the softened gelatin into
the plain custard until it has dissolved,
then stir in the remaining rum. Set
the pan in cold water until it reaches
room temperature.

10 ▲ With an electric mixer, beat
the egg whites and cream of tartar
until they hold stiff peaks. Add the
remaining sugar gradually, beating or
whisking thoroughly at each addition.

11 ▲ Fold the custard into the egg
whites, then spoon over the chocolate
mixture in the pie shell. Refrigerate
until set, about 2 hours.

12 Decorate the top with chocolate
curls. Keep the pie refrigerated until
ready to serve.

~ COOK'S TIP ~

To make chocolate curls, melt
8 oz (225 g) plain chocolate over
hot water, stir in 1 tablespoon of
vegetable fat and mould in a small
foil-lined loaf tin. For large curls,
soften the bar between your hands
and scrape off curls from the wide
side with a vegetable peeler; for
small curls, grate from the narrow
side using a box grater.

Velvety Mocha Tart

2 tsp instant espresso coffee

2 tbsp hot water

12 fl oz (350 ml) whipping cream

6 oz (170 g) plain chocolate

1 oz (30 g) bitter cooking chocolate

4 fl oz (125 ml) whipped cream, for decorating

chocolate-covered coffee beans, for decorating

FOR THE BASE

5 oz (140 g) chocolate wafers, crushed

2 tbsp caster sugar

2½ oz (70 g) butter, melted

1 ▲ For the base, mix the crushed chocolate wafers and sugar together, then stir in the melted butter.

2 Press the mixture evenly over the bottom and sides of a 9 in (23 cm) pie dish. Refrigerate until firm.

3 In a bowl, dissolve the coffee in the water and set aside.

4 Pour the cream into a mixing bowl. Set the bowl in hot water to warm the cream, bringing it closer to the temperature of the chocolate.

5 Melt both the chocolates in the top of a double boiler, or in a heatproof bowl set over a pan of hot water. Remove from the heat when nearly melted and stir to continue melting. Set the bottom of the pan in cool water to reduce the temperature. Be careful not to splash any water on the chocolate or it will become grainy.

6 ▲ With an electric mixer, whip the cream until it is lightly fluffy. Add the dissolved coffee and whip until the cream just holds its shape.

7 ▲ When the chocolate is at room temperature, fold it gently into the cream with a large metal spoon.

8 Pour into the chilled biscuit base and refrigerate until firm. To serve, pipe a ring of whipped cream rosettes around the edge, then place a chocolate-covered coffee bean in the centre of each rosette.

Brandy Alexander Tart

SERVES 8

4 fl oz (125 ml) cold water
1 tablespoon powdered gelatine
4 oz (115 g) sugar
3 eggs, separated
4 tablespoons brandy
4 tablespoons crème de cacao
pinch of salt
10 fl oz (300 ml) whipping cream
chocolate curls, for decorating
FOR THE BISCUIT CRUST
8 oz (225 g) digestive biscuits, crumbed
2½ oz (70 g) butter, melted
1 tablespoon sugar

1 Preheat the oven to 375°F/190°C/Gas 5.

2 For the crust, mix the biscuit crumbs with the butter and sugar in a bowl.

3 ▲ Press the crumbs evenly on to the bottom and sides of a 9 in (23 cm) tart tin. Bake until just brown, about 10 minutes. Cool on a rack.

4 Place the water in the top of a double boiler set over hot water. Sprinkle over the gelatine and leave to stand for 5 minutes to soften. Add half the sugar and the egg yolks. Whisk constantly over very low heat until the gelatine dissolves and the mixture thickens slightly. Do not allow the mixture to boil.

5 ▲ Remove from the heat and stir in the brandy and crème de cacao.

6 Set the pan over iced water and stir occasionally until it cools and thickens; it should not set firmly.

7 With an electric mixer, beat the egg whites and salt until they hold stiff peaks. Beat in the remaining sugar. Spoon a dollop of whites into the yolk mixture and fold in to lighten.

8 ▼ Pour the egg yolk mixture over the remaining whites and fold together.

9 Whip the cream until soft peaks form, then gently fold into the filling. Spoon into the baked biscuit case and chill until set, 3–4 hours. Decorate the top with chocolate curls before serving.

Glacé Fruit Pie

SERVES 10

1 tablespoon rum
2 oz (55 g) mixed glacé fruit, chopped
16 fl oz (450 ml) milk
4 teaspoons gelatin
3½ oz (100 g) sugar
½ teaspoon salt
3 eggs, separated
8 fl oz (250 ml) whipping cream
chocolate curls, for decorating

FOR THE CRUST

6 oz (170 g) digestive biscuits, crushed
2½ oz (70 g) butter, melted
1 tablespoon sugar

1 For the crust, mix the crushed digestive biscuits, butter and sugar. Press evenly and firmly over the bottom and side of a 9 in (23 cm) pie plate. Refrigerate until firm.

2 ▲ In a bowl, stir together the rum and glacé fruit. Set aside.

3 Pour 4 fl oz (125 ml) of the milk into a small bowl. Sprinkle over the gelatin and let stand 5 minutes to soften.

4 ▲ In the top of a double boiler, combine 1¾ oz (50 g) of the sugar, the remaining milk and salt. Stir in the gelatin mixture. Cook over hot water, stirring, until gelatin dissolves.

5 Whisk in the egg yolks and cook, stirring, until thick enough to coat a spoon. Do not boil. Pour the custard over the glacé fruit mixture. Set in a bowl of ice water to cool.

6 Whip the cream lightly. Set aside.

7 With an electric mixer, beat the egg whites until they hold soft peaks. Add the remaining sugar and beat just enough to blend. Fold in a large dollop of the egg whites into the cooled gelatin mixture. Pour into the remaining egg whites and carefully fold together. Fold in the cream.

8 ▲ Pour into the pie shell and chill until firm. Decorate the top with chocolate curls.

Chocolate Chiffon Pie

Serves 8

7 oz (200 g) plain chocolate

8 fl oz (250 ml) milk

1 tablespoon gelatin

3½ oz (100 g) sugar

2 extra-large eggs, separated

1 teaspoon vanilla essence

12 fl oz (350 ml) whipping cream

⅛ teaspoon salt

whipped cream and chocolate curls, for
 decorating

For the crust

7 oz (200 g) digestive biscuits,
 crushed

3 oz (85 g) butter, melted

1 Place a baking sheet in the oven
and preheat to 350°F/180°C/
Gas 4.

2 For the crust, mix the crushed
digestive biscuits and butter in a bowl.
Press evenly over the bottom and side
of a 9 in (23 cm) pie plate. Bake for 8
minutes. Let cool.

3 Chop the chocolate, then grate in a
food processor or blender. Set aside.

4 Place the milk in the top of a
double boiler. Sprinkle over the
gelatin. Let stand 5 minutes to soften.

5 ▲ Set the top of a double boiler
over hot water. Add 1½ oz (45 g)
sugar, the chocolate and egg yolks.
Stir until dissolved. Add the vanilla.

6 ▲ Set the top of the double boiler
in a bowl of ice and stir until the
mixture reaches room temperature.
Remove from the ice and set aside.

7 Whip the cream lightly. Set aside.
With an electric mixer, beat the egg
whites and salt until they hold soft
peaks. Add the remaining sugar and
beat only enough to blend.

8 Fold a dollop of egg whites into the
chocolate mixture, then pour back
into the whites and fold in.

9 ▲ Fold in the whipped cream and
pour into the pie shell. Put in the
freezer until just set, about 5 minutes.
If the centre sinks, fill with any
remaining mixture. Refrigerate for 3–4
hours. Decorate with whipped cream
and chocolate curls. Serve cold.

Chocolate Cheesecake Tart

SERVES 8

12 oz (350 g) cream cheese
4 tbsp whipping cream
8 oz (225 g) caster sugar
2 oz (55 g) cocoa powder
½ tsp ground cinnamon
3 eggs
whipped cream, for decorating
chocolate curls, for decorating
FOR THE BASE
3 oz (85 g) digestive biscuits, crushed
1½ oz (45 g) crushed amaretti biscuits (if unavailable, use extra crushed digestive biscuits)
3 oz (85 g) butter, melted

1 Preheat a baking sheet in the centre of a 350°F/180°C/Gas 4 oven.

2 For the base, mix the crushed biscuits and butter in a bowl.

3 ▲ With a spoon, press the mixture over the bottom and sides of a 9 in (23 cm) pie dish. Bake for 8 minutes. Let cool. Keep the oven on.

4 With an electric mixer, beat the cheese and cream together until smooth. Beat in the sugar, cocoa and cinnamon until blended.

5 ▼ Add the eggs, 1 at a time, beating just enough to blend.

6 Pour into the biscuit base and bake on the hot sheet for 25–30 minutes. The filling will sink down as it cools. Decorate with whipped cream and chocolate curls.

Frozen Strawberry Tart

SERVES 8

8 oz (225 g) cream cheese
8 fl oz (250 ml) soured cream
1 lb 4 oz (575 g) frozen strawberries, thawed and sliced
FOR THE BASE
4 oz (115 g) digestive biscuits, crushed
1 tbsp caster sugar
2½ oz (70 g) butter, melted

> **~ VARIATION ~**
>
> For Frozen Raspberry Tart, use raspberries in place of the strawberries and prepare the same way, or try other frozen fruit.

1 ▲ For the base, mix together the biscuits, sugar and butter.

2 Press the mixture evenly and firmly over the bottom and sides of a 9 in (23 cm) pie dish. Freeze until firm.

3 ▼ Blend together the cream cheese and soured cream. Reserve 6 tablespoons of the strawberries. Add the rest to the cream cheese mixture.

4 Pour the filling into the biscuit base and freeze 6–8 hours until firm. To serve, spoon some of the reserved berries and juice on top.

Chocolate Cheesecake Pie (top), Frozen Strawberry Tart

Kiwi Ricotta Cheese Tart

SERVES 8

3 oz (75 g) blanched almonds, ground
3½ oz (130 g) sugar
2 lb (900 g) ricotta cheese
8 fl oz (250 ml) whipping cream
1 egg and 3 egg yolks
1 tablespoon plain flour
pinch of salt
2 tablespoons rum
grated rind of 1 lemon
2½ tablespoons lemon juice
2 tablespoons honey
5 kiwi fruit
FOR THE PASTRY
5 oz (150 g) plain flour
1 tablespoon sugar
½ teaspoon salt
½ teaspoon baking powder
6 tablespoons butter
1 egg yolk
3–4 tablespoons whipping cream

1 For the pastry, mix together the flour, sugar, salt and baking powder in a large bowl. Cut the butter into cubes and gradually rub it into the pastry mixture. Mix in the egg yolk and cream. Stir in just enough to bind the pastry.

2 ▲ Transfer to a lightly floured surface, flatten slightly, wrap and refrigerate for 30 minutes. Preheat the oven to 425°F/220°C/Gas 7.

3 ▲ On a lightly floured surface, roll out the dough to a ⅛ in (3 mm) thickness. Transfer to a 9 in (23 cm) springform tin. Crimp the edge.

4 ▲ Prick the pastry with a fork. Line with greaseproof paper and fill with dried beans. Bake for 10 minutes. Remove the paper and beans and bake for 6–8 minutes more until golden. Leave to cool. Reduce the temperature to 350°F/180°C/Gas 4.

5 ▲ Mix the almonds with 1 tablespoon of the sugar in a food processor or blender.

6 Beat the ricotta until creamy. Add the cream, egg, yolks, remaining sugar, flour, salt, rum, lemon rind and 2 tablespoons of lemon juice. Combine.

7 ▲ Stir in the ground almonds until well blended.

8 Pour into a pastry case and bake for 1 hour. Chill, loosely covered for 2–3 hours. Unmould and put on a plate.

9 Combine the honey and remaining lemon juice for the glaze.

10 ▲ Peel the kiwis. Halve them lengthwise, then slice. Arrange the slices in rows across the top of the tart. Just before serving, brush with the honey glaze.

Apple Strudel

SERVES 10–12

3 oz (85 g) raisins
2 tbsp brandy
5 eating apples, such as Granny Smith or Cox's
3 large cooking apples
3½ oz (100 g) dark brown sugar
1 tsp ground cinnamon
grated rind and juice of 1 lemon
1 oz (30 g) dry breadcrumbs
2 oz (55 g) chopped pecans or walnuts
12 sheets frozen filo pastry, thawed
6 oz (170 g) butter, melted
icing sugar, for dusting

1 Soak the raisins in the brandy for at least 15 minutes.

2 ▼ Peel, core and thinly slice the apples. In a bowl, combine the sugar, cinnamon and lemon rind. Stir in the apples and half the breadcrumbs.

3 Add the raisins, nuts and lemon juice and stir until blended.

4 Preheat a 375°F/190°C/Gas 5 oven. Grease 2 baking sheets.

5 ▲ Carefully unfold the filo sheets. Keep the unused sheets covered with greaseproof paper. Lift off 1 sheet, place on a clean surface and brush with melted butter. Lay a second sheet on top and brush with butter. Continue until you have a stack of 6 buttered sheets.

6 Sprinkle a few tablespoons of breadcrumbs over the last sheet and spoon half the apple mixture at the bottom edge of the strip.

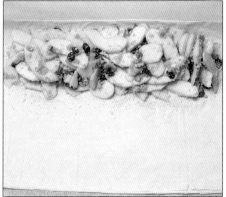

7 ▲ Starting at the apple-filled end, roll up the pastry, as for a Swiss roll. Place on a baking sheet, seam-side down, and carefully fold under the ends to seal. Repeat the procedure to make a second strudel. Brush both with butter.

8 Bake the strudels for 45 minutes. Let cool slightly. Using a small sieve, dust with a fine layer of icing sugar. Serve warm.

Cherry Strudel

SERVES 8

2½ oz (70 g) fresh breadcrumbs
6 oz (170 g) butter, melted
7 oz (200 g) sugar
1 tablespoon ground cinnamon
1 teaspoon grated lemon rind
1 lb (450 g) sour cherries, stoned
8 sheets filo pastry
icing sugar, for dusting

1 In a frying pan, lightly fry the fresh breadcrumbs in 2½ oz (70 g) of the melted butter until golden. Set aside to cool.

2 ▲ In a large mixing bowl, toss together the sugar, cinnamon and lemon rind.

3 Stir in the cherries.

4 Preheat the oven to 375°F/190°C/ Gas 5. Grease a baking sheet.

5 Carefully unfold the filo sheets. Keep the unused sheets covered with damp kitchen paper. Lift off one sheet, place on a flat surface lined with parchment paper. Brush the pastry with melted butter. Sprinkle about an eighth of the breadcrumbs evenly over the surface.

6 ▲ Lay a second sheet of filo on top, brush with butter and sprinkle with crumbs. Continue until you have a stack of 8 buttered, crumbed sheets.

7 Spoon the cherry mixture at the bottom edge of the strip. Starting at the cherry-filled end, roll up the dough as for a Swiss roll. Use the paper to help flip the strudel onto the baking sheet, seam-side down.

8 ▼ Carefully fold under the ends to seal in the fruit. Brush the top with any remaining butter.

9 Bake the strudel for 45 minutes. Let cool slightly. Using a small sieve, dust with a fine layer of icing sugar.

Mushroom Quiche

SERVES 8

1 lb (450 g) mushrooms

2 tablespoons olive oil

1 tablespoon butter

1 clove garlic, finely chopped

1 tablespoon lemon juice

salt and pepper

2 tablespoons finely chopped parsley

3 eggs

12 fl oz (300 ml) whipping cream

2¼ oz (60 g) Parmesan cheese, grated

FOR THE CRUST

6¼ oz (180 g) plain flour

½ teaspoon salt

3 oz (85 g) cold butter, cut into pieces

1½ oz (45 g) cold margarine, cut into pieces

3–4 tablespoons iced water

1 For the crust, sift the flour and salt into a bowl. Rub in the butter and margarine until the mixture resembles coarse breadcrumbs. Stir in just enough water to bind.

2 Gather into a ball, wrap in clear film and refrigerate for 20 minutes.

3 Preheat a baking sheet in a 375°F/190°C/Gas 5 oven.

4 Roll out the dough ⅛ in (3 mm) thick. Transfer to a 9 in (23 cm) tart tin and trim. Prick the base all over with a fork. Line with greaseproof paper and fill with dried beans. Bake for 12 minutes. Remove the paper and beans and continue baking until golden, about 5 minutes more.

5 ▲ Wipe the mushrooms with damp kitchen paper to remove any dirt. Trim the ends of the stalks, place on a cutting board, and slice thinly.

6 Heat the oil and butter in a frying pan. Stir in the mushrooms, garlic and lemon juice. Season with salt and pepper. Cook until the mushrooms render their liquid, then raise the heat and cook until dry.

7 ▼ Stir in the parsley and add more salt and pepper if necessary.

8 Whisk the eggs and cream together, then stir in the mushrooms. Sprinkle the cheese over the bottom of the prebaked shell and pour the mushroom filling over the top.

9 Bake until puffed and brown, about 30 minutes. Serve the quiche warm.

Bacon and Cheese Quiche

SERVES 8

4 oz (115 g) medium-thick bacon slices

3 eggs

12 fl oz (350 ml) whipping cream

3½ oz (100 g) Gruyère cheese, grated

⅛ teaspoon grated nutmeg

salt and pepper

FOR THE CRUST

6¼ oz (180 g) plain flour

½ teaspoon salt

3 oz (85 g) cold butter, cut into pieces

1½ oz (45 g) cold margarine, cut into pieces

3–4 tablespoons iced water

1 Make the crust as directed in steps 1–4 above. Maintain the oven temperature at 375°F/190°C/Gas 5.

2 ▲ Fry the bacon until crisp. Drain, then crumble into small pieces. Sprinkle in the pastry shell.

3 ▲ Beat together the eggs, cream, cheese, nutmeg, salt and pepper. Pour over the bacon and bake until puffed and brown, about 30 minutes. Serve the quiche warm.

Mushroom Quiche (top), Bacon and Cheese Quiche

Cheesy Tomato Quiche

SERVES 6–8

10 medium tomatoes

1 × 2 oz (55 g) can anchovy fillets, drained and finely chopped

4 fl oz (125 ml) whipping cream

7 oz (200 g) mature Cheddar cheese, grated

1 oz (30 g) wholemeal breadcrumbs

½ teaspoon dried thyme

salt and pepper

FOR THE CRUST

7½ oz (215 g) plain flour

4 oz (115 g) cold butter, cut into pieces

1 egg yolk

2–3 tablespoons iced water

1 Preheat the oven to 400°F/200°C/ Gas 6.

2 For the crust, sift the flour into a bowl. Rub in the butter with your fingertips until the mixture resembles coarse breadcrumbs.

3 ▲ With a fork, stir in the egg yolk and enough water to bind the dough.

4 Roll out the dough about ⅛ in (3 mm) thick and transfer to a 9 in (23 cm) tart tin. Refrigerate until needed.

5 ▲ Score the bottoms of the tomatoes. Plunge in boiling water for 1 minute. Remove and peel off the skin with a knife. Cut in quarters and remove the seeds with a spoon.

6 ▲ In a bowl, mix the anchovies and cream. Stir in the cheese.

7 Sprinkle the breadcrumbs in the tart. Arrange the tomatoes on top. Season with thyme, salt and pepper.

8 ▲ Spoon the cheese mixture on top. Bake until golden, 25–30 minutes. Serve warm.

Onion and Anchovy Tart

Serves 8

4 tablespoons olive oil

2 lb (900 g) onions, sliced

1 teaspoon dried thyme

salt and pepper

2–3 tomatoes, sliced

24 small black olives, stoned

1 × 2 oz (55 g) can anchovy fillets, drained and sliced

6 sun-dried tomatoes, cut into slivers

For the crust

6¼ oz (180 g) plain flour

½ teaspoon salt

4 oz (115 g) cold butter, cut into pieces

1 egg yolk

2–3 tablespoons iced water

3 ▲ Heat the oil in a frying pan. Add the onions, thyme and seasoning. Cook over low heat, covered, for 25 minutes. Uncover and continue cooking until soft. Let cool. Preheat the oven to 400°F/200°C/Gas 6.

4 ▼ Spoon the onions into the tart shell and top with the tomato slices. Arrange the olives in rows. Make a lattice pattern, alternating lines of anchovies and sun-dried tomatoes. Bake until golden, 20–25 minutes.

1 ▲ For the crust, sift the flour and salt into a bowl. Rub in the butter with your fingertips until the mixture resembles coarse breadcrumbs. Stir in the yolk and enough water to bind.

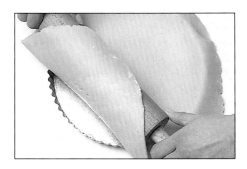

2 ▲ Roll out the dough about ⅛ in (3 mm) thick. Transfer to a 9 in (23 cm) tart tin and trim the edge. Refrigerate until needed.

Ricotta and Basil Tart

SERVES 8–10

2 oz (55 g) basil leaves

1 oz (30 g) flat-leaf parsley

4 fl oz (125 ml) extra-virgin olive oil

salt and pepper

2 eggs

1 egg yolk

1 lb 12 oz (800 g) ricotta cheese

3½ oz (100 g) black olives, stoned

2¼ oz (60 g) Parmesan cheese, freshly grated

FOR THE CRUST

6½ oz (180 g) plain flour

½ teaspoon salt

3 oz (85 g) cold butter, cut into pieces

1½ oz (45 g) cold margarine, cut into pieces

3–4 tablespoons iced water

1 ▲ For the crust, combine the flour and salt in a bowl. Add the butter and margarine.

2 Rub in with your fingertips until the mixture resembles coarse breadcrumbs. With a fork, stir in just enough water to bind the dough. Gather into a ball, wrap in clear film, and refrigerate for at least 20 minutes.

3 Preheat a baking sheet in a 375°F/190°C/Gas 5 oven.

4 Roll out the dough ⅛ in (3 mm) thick and transfer to a 10 in (25 cm) tart tin. Prick the base with a fork and line with greaseproof. Fill with dried beans and bake for 12 minutes. Remove the paper and beans and bake until golden, 3–5 minutes more. Lower the heat to 350°F/180°C/Gas 4.

5 ▲ In a food processor, combine the basil, parsley and olive oil. Season well with salt and pepper and process until finely chopped.

6 In a bowl, whisk the eggs and yolk to blend. Gently fold in the ricotta.

7 ▲ Fold in the basil mixture and olives until well combined. Stir in the Parmesan and adjust the seasoning.

8 Pour into the prebaked shell and bake until set, 30–35 minutes.

Pennsylvania Dutch Ham and Apple Pie

SERVES 6–8

5 tart cooking apples
4 tablespoons light brown sugar
1 tablespoon plain flour
pinch of ground cloves
pinch of ground black pepper
6 oz (170 g) sliced cooked ham
1 oz (30 g) butter or margarine
4 tablespoons whipping cream
1 egg yolk
FOR THE PASTRY
8 oz (225 g) plain flour
½ teaspoon salt
3 oz (85 g) cold butter, cut into pieces
2 oz (55 g) cold margarine, cut into pieces
4–8 tablespoons iced water

1 For the pastry, sift the flour and salt into a large bowl. Rub in the butter and margarine until the mixture resembles coarse crumbs. Stir in enough water to bind together, gather into 2 balls, and wrap in clear film. Refrigerate for about 20 minutes. Preheat the oven to 425°F/220°C/Gas 7.

2 ▲ Quarter, core, peel and thinly slice the apples. Place in a bowl and toss with the sugar, flour, cloves and pepper to coat evenly. Set aside.

3 Roll out one dough ball thinly and line a 10 in (25 cm) pie tin, letting the excess pastry hang over the edge.

4 Arrange half the ham slices in the bottom of the pastry case. Top with a ring of spiced apple slices, then dot with half the butter or margarine.

5 ▲ Repeat the layers, finishing with apples. Dot with butter or margarine. Pour over 3 tablespoons of the cream.

6 Roll out the remaining pastry to make a lid. Place it on top, fold the top edge under the bottom and press.

7 ▲ Roll out the pastry scraps and cut out decorative shapes. Arrange on top of the pie. Scallop the edge, using your fingers and a fork. Cut steam vents. Mix the egg yolk and remaining cream and brush on top to glaze.

8 Bake for 10 minutes. Reduce the heat to 350°F/180°C/Gas 4 and bake until golden, 30–35 minutes more. Serve hot.

CAKES & GATEAUX

~

As delicious as they are beautiful, these cakes and gâteaux are perfect to serve at teatime or for dessert. Some delightful party cakes make special occasions memorable.

Angel Cake

SERVES 12–14

4½ oz (125 g) sifted plain flour
2 tablespoons cornflour
10½ oz (300 g) caster sugar
10–11 oz (285–310 g) egg whites (about 10–11 eggs)
1¼ teaspoons cream of tartar
¼ teaspoon salt
1 teaspoon vanilla essence
¼ teaspoon almond essence
icing sugar, for dusting

1 Preheat the oven to 325°F/170°C/Gas 3.

2 ▼ Sift the flours before measuring, then sift them 4 times with 3½ oz (100 g) of the sugar.

3 With an electric mixer, beat the egg whites until foamy. Sift over the cream of tartar and salt and continue to beat until the whites hold soft peaks when the beaters are lifted.

4 ▲ Add the remaining sugar in 3 batches, beating well after each addition. Stir in the vanilla and almond essences.

5 ▲ Add the flour mixture, in 2 batches, and fold in with a large metal spoon after each addition.

6 Transfer to an ungreased 10 in (25 cm) tube tin and bake until just browned on top, about 1 hour.

7 ▲ Turn the tin upside down onto a cake rack and let cool for 1 hour. If the cake does not turn out, run a knife around the edge to loosen it. Invert on a serving plate.

8 When cool, lay a star-shaped template on top of the cake, sift over icing sugar and remove template.

Marbled Ring Cake

SERVES 16

4 oz (115 g) plain chocolate
12 oz (350 g) plain flour
1 tsp baking powder
1 lb (450 g) butter, at room temperature
1 lb 10 oz (740 g) caster sugar
1 tbsp vanilla essence
10 eggs, at room temperature
icing sugar, for dusting

1 ▲ Preheat a 350°F/180°C/Gas 4 oven. Line a 10 × 4 in (25 × 10 cm) ring mould with greaseproof paper and grease the paper. Dust with flour.

2 ▲ Melt the chocolate in the top of a double boiler, or in a heatproof bowl set over a pan of hot water. Stir occasionally. Set aside.

3 In a bowl, sift together the flour and baking powder. In another bowl, cream the butter, sugar and vanilla with an electric mixer until light and fluffy. Add the eggs, 2 at a time, then gradually incorporate the flour mixture on low speed.

4 ▲ Spoon half of the mixture into the prepared tin.

5 ▲ Stir the chocolate into the remaining mixture, then spoon into the tin. With a metal spatula, swirl the mixtures for a marbled effect.

6 Bake until a skewer inserted in the centre comes out clean, about 1 hour 45 minutes. Cover with foil halfway through baking. Let stand 15 minutes, then unmould and transfer to a cooling rack. To serve, dust with icing sugar.

Coffee-Iced Ring

SERVES 16

10 oz (285 g) plain flour
1 tbsp baking powder
1 tsp salt
12 oz (350 g) caster sugar
4 fl oz (125 ml) vegetable oil
7 eggs, at room temperature, separated
6 fl oz (175 ml) cold water
2 tsp vanilla essence
2 tsp grated lemon rind
½ tsp cream of tartar
FOR THE ICING
5½ oz (165 g) unsalted butter, at room temperature
1 lb 4 oz (575 g) icing sugar
4 tsp instant coffee dissolved in 4 tbsp hot water

1 Preheat a 325°F/170°C/Gas 3 oven.

2 ▼ Sift the flour, baking powder and salt into a bowl. Stir in 8 oz (225 g) of the sugar. Make a well in the centre and add in the following order: oil, egg yolks, water, vanilla and lemon rind. Beat with a whisk or metal spoon until smooth.

3 With an electric mixer, beat the egg whites with the cream of tartar until they hold soft peaks. Add the remaining 4 oz (115 g) of sugar and beat until they hold stiff peaks.

4 ▲ Pour the flour mixture over the whites in 3 batches, folding well after each addition.

5 Transfer the mixture to a 10 × 4 in (25 × 10 cm) ring mould and bake until the top springs back when touched lightly, about 1 hour.

6 ▲ When baked, remove from the oven and immediately hang the cake upside-down over the neck of a funnel or a narrow bottle. Let cool. To remove the cake, run a knife around the inside to loosen, then turn the tin over and tap the sides sharply. Invert the cake onto a serving plate.

7 For the icing, beat together the butter and icing sugar with an electric mixer until smooth. Add the coffee and beat until fluffy. With a metal spatula, spread over the sides and top of the cake.

Spice Cake with Cream Cheese Frosting

SERVES 10–12

10 fl oz (300 ml) milk
2 tablespoons golden syrup
2 teaspoons vanilla essence
3 oz (85 g) walnuts, chopped
6 oz (170 g) butter, at room temperature
10½ oz (300 g) sugar
1 egg, at room temperature
3 egg yolks, at room temperature
10 oz (285 g) plain flour
1 tablespoon baking powder
1 teaspoon grated nutmeg
1 teaspoon ground cinnamon
½ teaspoon ground cloves
¼ teaspoon ground ginger
¼ teaspoon ground allspice
FOR THE FROSTING
6 oz (170 g) cream cheese
1 oz (30 g) unsalted butter
7 oz (200 g) icing sugar
2 tablespoons finely chopped stem ginger
2 tablespoons syrup from stem ginger
stem ginger pieces, for decorating

1 Preheat a 350°F/180°C/Gas 4 oven. Line 3 8 in (20 cm) cake tins with greaseproof paper and grease. In a bowl, combine the milk, golden syrup, vanilla and walnuts.

2 ▼ With an electric mixer, cream the butter and sugar until light and fluffy. Beat in the egg and egg yolks. Add the milk mixture and stir well.

3 Sift together the flour, baking powder and spices 3 times.

4 ▲ Add the flour mixture in 4 batches, and fold in carefully after each addition.

5 Divide the cake mixture between the tins. Bake until the cakes spring back when touched lightly, about 25 minutes. Let stand 5 minutes, then turn out and cool on a rack.

6 ▼ For the frosting, combine all the ingredients and beat with an electric mixer. Spread the frosting between the layers and over the top. Decorate with pieces of stem ginger.

Caramel Layer Cake

SERVES 8–10

10 oz (285 g) plain flour
1½ teaspoons baking powder
6 oz (170 g) butter, at room temperature
5½ oz (150 g) caster sugar
4 eggs, at room temperature, beaten
1 teaspoon vanilla essence
8 tablespoons milk
whipped cream, for decorating
caramel threads, for decorating (optional, see below)

FOR THE FROSTING

10½ oz (300 g) dark brown sugar
8 fl oz (250 ml) milk
1 oz (30 g) unsalted butter
3–5 tablespoons whipping cream

1 Preheat a 350°F/180°C/Gas 4 oven. Line 2 8 in (20 cm) cake tins with greaseproof paper and grease lightly.

2 ▲ Sift the flour and baking powder together 3 times. Set aside.

~ **COOK'S TIP** ~

To make caramel threads, combine 2½ oz (70 g) sugar and 2 fl oz (65 ml) water in a heavy saucepan. Boil until light brown. Dip the pan in cold water to halt cooking. Trail from a spoon on an oiled baking sheet.

---

3 With an electric mixer, cream the butter and caster sugar until light and fluffy.

4 ▲ Slowly mix in the beaten eggs. Add the vanilla. Fold in the flour mixture, alternating with the milk.

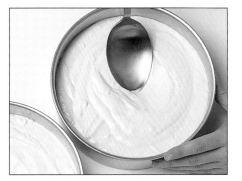

5 ▲ Divide the batter between the prepared tins and spread evenly, hollowing out the centres slightly.

6 Bake until the cakes pull away from the sides of the tin, about 30 minutes. Let stand 5 minutes, then turn out and cool on a rack.

7 ▲ For the frosting, combine the brown sugar and milk in a saucepan.

8 Bring to the boil, cover and cook for 3 minutes. Remove lid and continue to boil, without stirring, until the mixture reaches 238°F/119°C (soft ball stage) on a sugar thermometer.

9 ▲ Immediately remove the pan from the heat and add the butter, but do not stir it in. Let cool until lukewarm, then beat until the mixture is smooth and creamy.

10 Stir in enough cream to obtain a spreadable consistency. If necessary, refrigerate to thicken more.

11 ▲ Spread a layer of frosting on top of one cake. Sandwich with the second cake, then spread the top and sides with the rest of the frosting and smooth the surface.

12 To decorate, pipe whipped cream rosettes around the edge. If using, place a mound of caramel threads in the centre before serving.

Lady Baltimore Cake

SERVES 8–10

10 oz (285 g) plain flour
2½ teaspoons baking powder
½ teaspoon salt
4 eggs
12 oz (350 g) sugar
grated rind of 1 large orange
8 fl oz (250 ml) fresh orange juice
8 fl oz (250 ml) vegetable oil
18 pecan halves, for decorating
FOR THE FROSTING
2 egg whites
12 oz (350 g) sugar
5 tablespoons cold water
¼ teaspoon cream of tartar
1 teaspoon vanilla essence
2 oz (55 g) pecans, finely chopped
3 oz (85 g) raisins, chopped
3 dried figs, finely chopped

1 Preheat the oven to 350°F/180°C/Gas 4. Grease 2 9 in (23 cm) round cake tins and line with greaseproof paper. Grease the paper. In a bowl, sift together the flour, baking powder and salt. Set aside.

2 ▲ With an electric mixer, beat the eggs and sugar until thick and lemon-coloured. Beat in the orange rind and juice, then the oil.

3 On low speed, beat in the flour mixture in 3 batches. Divide the cake mixture between the tins.

4 ▲ Bake until a skewer inserted in the centre comes out clean, about 30 minutes. Leave to stand for 15 minutes, then run a knife around the inside of the cakes and transfer them to racks to cool completely.

5 ▲ For the frosting, combine the egg whites, sugar, water and cream of tartar in the top of a double boiler, or in a heatproof bowl set over boiling water. With an electric mixer, beat until glossy and thick. Off the heat, add the vanilla essence and continue beating until thick. Fold in the pecans, raisins and figs.

6 Spread a layer of frosting on top of one cake. Sandwich with the second cake, then spread the top and sides with the rest of the frosting. Arrange the pecan halves on top.

Carrot Cake

SERVES 12

1 lb (450 g) carrots, peeled
6 oz (170 g) plain flour
2 tsp baking powder
½ tsp bicarbonate of soda
1 tsp salt
2 tsp ground cinnamon
4 eggs
2 tsp vanilla essence
4 oz (115 g) dark brown sugar
2 oz (55 g) caster sugar
10 fl oz (300 ml) sunflower oil
4 oz (115 g) finely chopped walnuts
3 oz (85 g) raisins
walnut halves, for decorating (optional)
FOR THE ICING
3 oz (85 g) unsalted butter, at room temperature
12 oz (350 g) icing sugar
2 fl oz (65 ml) maple syrup

1 Preheat a 350°F/180°C/Gas 4 oven. Line an 11 × 8 in (28 × 20 cm) tin with greaseproof paper and grease.

2 ▲ Grate the carrots and set aside.

3 Sift the flour, baking powder, bicarbonate of soda, salt and cinnamon into a bowl. Set aside.

4 With an electric mixer, beat the eggs until blended. Add the vanilla, sugars and oil; beat to incorporate. Add the dry ingredients, in 3 batches, folding in well after each addition.

5 ▲ Add the carrots, walnuts and raisins and fold in thoroughly.

6 Pour the mixture into the prepared tin and bake until the cake springs back when touched lightly, 40–45 minutes. Let stand 10 minutes, then unmould and transfer to a rack.

7 ▼ For the icing, cream the butter with half the icing sugar until soft. Add the syrup, then beat in the remaining sugar until blended.

8 Spread the icing over the top of the cake. Using the tip of a palette knife, make decorative ridges in the icing. Cut into squares. Decorate with walnut halves, if wished.

Cranberry Upside-Down Cake

SERVES 8

12–14 oz (350–400 g) fresh cranberries
2 oz (55 g) butter
5 oz (140 g) sugar
FOR THE CAKE MIXTURE
2½ oz (70 g) plain flour
1 teaspoon baking powder
3 eggs
4 oz (115 g) sugar
grated rind of 1 orange
1½ oz (45 g) butter, melted

1 Preheat the oven to 350°F/180°C/ Gas 4. Place a baking sheet on the middle shelf of the oven.

2 Wash the cranberries and pat dry. Thickly smear the butter on the bottom and sides of a 9 x 2 in (23 x 5 cm) round cake tin. Add the sugar and swirl the tin to coat evenly.

3 ▲ Add the cranberries and spread in an even layer over the bottom of the tin.

4 For the cake mixture, sift the flour and baking powder twice. Set aside.

5 ▲ Combine the eggs, sugar and orange rind in a heatproof bowl set over a pan of hot but not boiling water. With an electric mixer, beat until the eggs leave a ribbon trail when the beaters are lifted.

6 Add the flour mixture in 3 batches, folding in well after each addition. Gently fold in the melted butter, then pour over the cranberries.

7 Bake for 40 minutes. Leave to cool for 5 minutes, then run a knife around the inside edge to loosen.

8 ▲ While the cake is still warm, invert a plate on top of the tin. Protecting your hands with oven gloves, hold plate and tin firmly and turn them both over quickly. Lift off the tin carefully.

Pineapple Upside-Down Cake

SERVES 8

4 oz (115 g) butter
7 oz (200 g) dark brown sugar
16 oz (450 g) canned pineapple slices, drained
4 eggs, separated
grated rind of 1 lemon
⅛ tsp salt
4 oz (115 g) caster sugar
3 oz (85 g) plain flour
1 tsp baking powder

1 Preheat a 350°F/180°C/Gas 4 oven.

2 Melt the butter in a 10 in (25 cm) ovenproof cast-iron frying pan. Remove 1 tablespoon of the melted butter and set aside.

3 ▲ Add the brown sugar to the pan and stir until blended. Place the drained pineapple slices on top in one layer. Set aside.

~ **VARIATION** ~

For Dried Apricot Upside-Down Cake, replace the pineapple slices with 8 oz (225 g) of dried apricots. If they need softening, simmer the apricots in about 4 fl oz (125 ml) orange juice until plump and soft. Drain the apricots and discard any remaining cooking liquid.

4 In a bowl, whisk together the egg yolks, reserved butter and lemon rind until well blended. Set aside.

5 ▼ With an electric mixer, beat the egg whites with the salt until stiff. Fold in the caster sugar, 2 tablespoons at a time. Fold in the egg yolk mixture.

6 Sift the flour and baking powder together. Carefully fold into the egg mixture in 3 batches.

7 ▲ Pour the mixture over the pineapple and smooth level.

8 Bake until a skewer inserted in the centre comes out clean, about 30 minutes.

9 While still hot, place a serving plate on top of the pan, bottom-side up. Holding them tightly together with oven gloves, quickly flip over. Serve hot or cold.

Lemon Coconut Layer Cake

SERVES 8–10

5 oz (140 g) plain flour
⅛ teaspoon salt
8 eggs
12¾ oz (375 g) caster sugar
1 tablespoon grated orange rind
grated rind of 2 lemons
juice of 1 lemon
2½ oz (70 g) sweetened, shredded coconut
2 tablespoons cornflour
8 fl oz (250 ml) water
3 oz (85 g) butter
FOR THE FROSTING
4 oz (115 g) unsalted butter
4 oz (115 g) icing sugar
grated rind of 1 lemon
6–8 tablespoons lemon juice
4 oz (115 g) sweetened shredded coconut

1 Preheat a 350°F/180°C/Gas 4 oven. Line 3 8 in (20 cm) cake tins with greaseproof paper and grease. In a bowl, sift together the flour and salt and set aside.

2 ▲ Place 6 of the eggs in a large heatproof bowl set over hot water. With an electric mixer, beat until frothy. Gradually beat in 5½ oz (150 g) caster sugar until the mixture doubles in volume and leaves a ribbon trail when the beaters are lifted, about 10 minutes.

3 ▲ Remove the bowl from the hot water. Fold in the orange rind, half the grated lemon rind and 1 tablespoon of the lemon juice until blended. Fold in the coconut.

4 Sift over the flour mixture in 3 batches, folding in thoroughly after each addition.

5 ▲ Divide the mixture between the prepared tins.

6 Bake until the cakes pull away from the sides of the tins, 25–30 minutes. Let stand 3–5 minutes, then turn out to cool on a rack.

7 In a bowl, blend the cornflour with a little cold water to dissolve. Whisk in the remaining eggs just until blended. Set aside.

8 ▲ In a saucepan, combine the remaining lemon rind and juice, the water, remaining sugar and butter.

9 Over a moderate heat, bring the mixture to the boil. Whisk in the eggs and cornstarch mixture, and return to the boil. Whisk continuously until thick, about 5 minutes. Remove from the heat. Cover with clear film to stop a skin forming and set aside.

10 ▲ For the frosting, cream the butter and icing sugar until smooth. Stir in the lemon rind and enough lemon juice to obtain a thick, spreadable consistency.

11 Sandwich the 3 cake layers with the lemon custard mixture. Spread the frosting over the top and sides. Cover the cake with the coconut, pressing it in gently.

Lemon Yogurt Ring

Serves 12

8 oz (225 g) butter, at room temperature
10½ oz (300 g) caster sugar
4 eggs, at room temperature, separated
2 teaspoons grated lemon rind
3 fl oz (85 ml) lemon juice
8 fl oz (250 ml) plain yogurt
10 oz (285 g) plain flour
2 teaspoons baking powder
1 teaspoon bicarbonate of soda
½ teaspoon salt
FOR THE GLAZE
4 oz (115 g) icing sugar
2 tablespoons lemon juice
3–4 tablespoons plain yogurt

1 Preheat a 350°F/180°C/Gas 4 oven. Grease a 4⅔ pt (3 litre) bundt or fluted tube tin and dust with flour.

2 With an electric mixer, cream the butter and caster sugar until light and fluffy. Add the egg yolks, 1 at a time, beating well after each addition.

3 ▲ Add the lemon rind, juice and yogurt and stir to blend.

4 Sift together the flour, baking powder and bicarbonate of soda. In another bowl, beat the egg whites and salt until they hold stiff peaks.

5 ▲ Fold the dry ingredients into the butter mixture, then fold in a dollop of egg whites. Fold in the remaining whites until blended.

6 Pour into the tin and bake until a skewer inserted in the centre comes out clean, about 50 minutes. Let stand 15 minutes, then turn out and cool on a rack.

7 For the glaze, sift the icing sugar into a bowl. Stir in the lemon juice and just enough yogurt to make a smooth glaze.

8 ▲ Set the cooled cake on the rack over a sheet of greaseproof paper or a baking sheet. Pour over the glaze and let it drip down the sides. Allow the glaze to set before serving.

Soured Cream Crumble Cake

SERVES 12–14

4 oz (115 g) butter, at room temperature
4½ oz (125 g) caster sugar
3 eggs, at room temperature
7½ oz (215 g) plain flour
1 teaspoon bicarbonate of soda
1 teaspoon baking powder
8 fl oz (250 ml) soured cream
FOR THE TOPPING
8 oz (225 g) dark brown sugar
2 teaspoons ground cinnamon
4 oz (115 g) walnuts, finely chopped
2 oz (55 g) cold butter, cut into pieces

1 Preheat a 350°F/180°C/Gas 4 oven. Line the bottom of a 9 in (23 cm) square cake tin with greaseproof paper and grease.

2 ▲ For the topping, place the brown sugar, cinnamon and walnuts in a bowl. Mix with your fingertips, then add the butter and continue working with your fingertips until the mixture resembles breadcrumbs.

3 To make the cake, cream the butter with an electric mixer until soft. Add the sugar and continue beating until the mixture is light and fluffy.

4 Add the eggs, 1 at a time, beating well after each addition.

5 In another bowl, sift the flour, bicarbonate of soda and baking powder together 3 times.

6 ▲ Fold the dry ingredients into the butter mixture in 3 batches, alternating with the soured cream. Fold until blended after each addition.

7 ▲ Pour half of the batter into the prepared tin and sprinkle over half of the walnut crumb topping mixture.

8 Pour the remaining batter on top and sprinkle over the remaining walnut crumb mixture.

9 Bake until browned, 60–70 minutes. Let stand 5 minutes, then turn out and cool on a rack.

Plum Crumble Cake

SERVES 8–10

5 oz (140 g) butter or margarine, at room temperature

5 oz (140 g) caster sugar

4 eggs, at room temperature

1½ tsp vanilla essence

5 oz (140 g) plain flour

1 tsp baking powder

1½ lb (700 g) red plums, halved and stoned

FOR THE TOPPING

4 oz (115 g) plain flour

4½ oz (130 g) light brown sugar

1½ tsp ground cinnamon

3 oz (85 g) butter, cut in pieces

1 Preheat a 350°F/180°C/Gas 4 oven.

2 For the topping, combine the flour, light brown sugar and cinnamon in a bowl. Add the butter and work the mixture lightly with your fingertips until it resembles coarse breadcrumbs. Set aside.

3 ▲ Line a 10 × 2 in (25 × 5 cm) tin with greaseproof paper and grease.

4 Cream the butter and sugar until light and fluffy.

5 ▲ Beat in the eggs, 1 at a time. Stir in the vanilla.

6 In a bowl, sift together the flour and baking powder, then fold into the butter mixture in 3 batches.

7 ▲ Pour the mixture into the tin. Arrange the plums on top.

8 ▲ Sprinkle the topping over the plums in an even layer.

9 Bake until a skewer inserted in the centre comes out clean, about 45 minutes. Let cool in the tin.

10 To serve, run a knife around the inside edge and invert onto a plate. Invert again onto a serving plate so the topping is right-side up.

~ **VARIATION** ~

This cake can also be made with the same quantity of apricots, peeled if preferred, or stoned cherries, or use a mixture of fruit, such as red or yellow plums, greengages and apricots.

Peach Torte

SERVES 8

4 oz (115 g) plain flour
1 teaspoon baking powder
pinch of salt
4 oz (115 g) unsalted butter, at room temperature
6 oz (170 g) sugar
2 eggs, at room temperature
6–7 peaches
sugar and lemon juice, for sprinkling
whipped cream, for serving (optional)

1 Preheat the oven to 350°F/180°C/ Gas 4. Grease a 10 in (25 cm) springform tin.

2 ▲ Sift together the flour, baking powder and salt. Set aside.

3 With an electric mixer, cream the butter and sugar until light and fluffy. Beat in the eggs, then fold in the dry ingredients until blended.

4 ▲ Spoon the mixture into the tin and smooth it to make an even layer over the bottom.

5 ▼ To skin the peaches, drop several at a time into a pan of gently boiling water. Boil for 10 seconds, then remove with a slotted spoon. Peel off the skin with the aid of a sharp knife. Cut the peaches in half and discard the stones.

6 ▲ Arrange the peach halves on top of the mixture. Sprinkle lightly with sugar and lemon juice.

7 Bake until golden brown and set, 50–60 minutes. Serve warm, with whipped cream, if liked.

Apple Ring Cake

SERVES 12

7 eating apples, such as Cox's or Granny Smith
12 fl oz (350 ml) vegetable oil
1 lb (450 g) caster sugar
3 eggs
15 oz (420 g) plain flour
1 tsp salt
1 tsp bicarbonate of soda
1 tsp ground cinnamon
1 tsp vanilla essence
4 oz (115 g) chopped walnuts
6 oz (170 g) raisins
icing sugar, for dusting

1 Preheat a 350°F/180°C/Gas 4 oven. Grease a 9 in (23 cm) ring mould.

2 ▲ Quarter, peel, core and slice the apples into a bowl. Set aside.

3 With an electric mixer, beat the oil and sugar together until blended. Add the eggs and continue beating until the mixture is creamy.

4 Sift together the flour, salt, bicarbonate of soda and cinnamon.

5 ▼ Fold the flour mixture into the egg mixture with the vanilla. Stir in the apples, walnuts and raisins.

6 Pour into the tin and bake until the cake springs back when touched lightly, about 1¼ hours. Let stand 15 minutes, then unmould and transfer to a cooling rack. Dust with a layer of icing sugar before serving.

Orange Cake

SERVES 6

6 oz (170 g) plain flour
1½ tsp baking powder
⅛ tsp salt
4 oz (115 g) butter or margarine
4 oz (115 g) caster sugar
grated rind of 1 large orange
2 eggs, at room temperature
2 tbsp milk
FOR THE SYRUP AND DECORATION
4 oz (115 g) caster sugar
8 fl oz (250 ml) fresh orange juice, strained
3 orange slices, for decorating

1 Preheat a 350°F/180°C/Gas 4 oven. Line an 8 in (20 cm) cake tin with greaseproof paper and grease the paper.

2 ▲ Sift the flour, salt and baking powder onto greaseproof paper.

3 With an electric mixer, cream the butter or margarine until soft. Add the sugar and orange rind and continue beating until light and fluffy. Beat in the eggs, 1 at a time. Fold in the flour in 3 batches, then add the milk.

4 Spoon into the tin and bake until the cake pulls away from the sides, about 30 minutes. Remove from the oven but leave in the tin.

5 Meanwhile, for the syrup, dissolve the sugar in the orange juice over a low heat. Add the orange slices and simmer for 10 minutes. Remove and drain. Let the syrup cool.

6 ▲ Prick the cake all over with a fine skewer. Pour the syrup over the hot cake. It may seem at first that there is too much syrup for the cake to absorb, but it will soak it all up. Unmould when completely cooled and decorate with small triangles of the orange slices arranged on top.

Apple Ring Cake (top), Orange Cake

Orange and Walnut Swiss Roll

SERVES 8

4 eggs, separated

4 oz (115 g) caster sugar

4 oz (115 g) very finely chopped walnuts

⅛ tsp cream of tartar

⅛ tsp salt

icing sugar, for dusting

FOR THE FILLING

10 fl oz (300 ml) whipping cream

1 tbsp caster sugar

grated rind of 1 orange

1 tbsp orange liqueur, such as Grand
   Marnier

1 Preheat a 350°F/180°C/Gas 4 oven.
Line a 12 × 9½ in (30 × 24 cm) Swiss
roll tin with greaseproof paper and
grease the paper.

2 With an electric mixer, beat the
egg yolks and sugar until thick.

3 ▲ Stir in the walnuts.

4 In another bowl, beat the egg
whites with the cream of tartar and
salt until they hold stiff peaks. Fold
gently but thoroughly into the
walnut mixture.

5 Pour the mixture into the prepared
tin and spread level with a spatula.
Bake for 15 minutes.

6 Run a knife along the inside edge to
loosen, then invert the cake onto a
sheet of greaseproof paper dusted with
icing sugar.

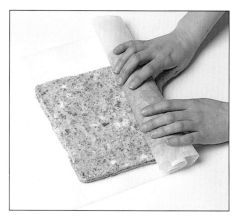

7 ▲ Peel off the baking paper. Roll
up the cake while it is still warm with
the help of the sugared paper. Set
aside to cool.

8 For the filling, whip the cream
until it holds soft peaks. Stir together
the caster sugar and orange rind, then
fold into the whipped cream. Add the
liqueur.

9 ▲ Gently unroll the cake. Spread
the inside with a layer of orange
whipped cream, then re-roll. Keep
refrigerated until ready to serve. Dust
the top with icing sugar just before
serving.

Chocolate Swiss Roll

SERVES 10

8 oz (225 g) plain chocolate
3 tbsp water
2 tbsp rum, brandy or strong coffee
7 eggs, separated
6 oz (170 g) caster sugar
⅛ tsp salt
12 fl oz (350 ml) whipping cream
icing sugar, for dusting

1 Preheat a 350°F/180°C/Gas 4 oven. Line a 15 × 13 in (38 × 33 cm) Swiss roll tin with greaseproof paper and grease the paper.

2 ▲ Combine the chocolate, water and rum or other flavouring in the top of a double boiler, or in a heatproof bowl set over hot water. Heat until melted. Set aside.

3 With an electric mixer, beat the egg yolks and sugar until thick.

4 ▲ Stir in the melted chocolate.

5 In another bowl, beat the egg whites and salt until they hold stiff peaks. Fold a large dollop of egg whites into the yolk mixture to lighten it, then carefully fold in the rest of the whites.

6 ▼ Pour the mixture into the pan; smooth evenly with a metal spatula.

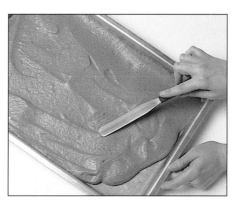

7 Bake for 15 minutes. Remove from the oven, cover with greaseproof paper and a damp cloth. Let stand for 1–2 hours.

8 With an electric mixer, whip the cream until stiff. Set aside.

9 Run a knife along the inside edge to loosen, then invert the cake onto a sheet of greaseproof paper that has been dusted with icing sugar.

10 Peel off the baking paper. Spread with an even layer of whipped cream, then roll up the cake with the help of the sugared paper.

11 Refrigerate for several hours. Before serving, dust with an even layer of icing sugar.

Chocolate Frosted Layer Cake

SERVES 8

8 oz (225 g) butter or margarine, at room temperature
10½ oz (300 g) sugar
4 eggs, at room temperature, separated
2 teaspoons vanilla essence
13½ oz (385 g) plain flour
2 teaspoons baking powder
⅛ teaspoon salt
8 fl oz (250 ml) milk
FOR THE FROSTING
5 oz (140 g) plain chocolate
4 fl oz (125 ml) soured cream
⅛ teaspoon salt

1 Preheat a 350°F/180°C/Gas 4 oven. Line 2 8 in (20 cm) round cake tins with greaseproof and grease. Dust the tins with flour and shake to distribute evenly. Tap to dislodge excess flour.

2 With an electric mixer, cream the butter or margarine until soft. Gradually add the sugar and continue beating until light and fluffy.

3 ▲ Lightly beat the egg yolks, then mix into the creamed butter and sugar with the vanilla.

4 Sift the flour with the baking powder 3 times. Set aside.

5 In another bowl, beat the egg whites with the salt until they hold stiff peaks. Set aside.

6 ▲ Gently fold the dry ingredients into the butter mixture in 3 batches, alternating with the milk.

7 Add a large dollop of the whites and fold in to lighten the mixture. Carefully fold in the remaining whites until just blended.

8 Divide the batter between the tins and bake until the cakes pull away from the sides of the tins, about 30 minutes. Let stand 5 minutes. Turn out and cool on a rack.

9 ▲ For the frosting, melt the chocolate in the top of a double boiler or a bowl set over hot water. When cool, stir in the soured cream and salt.

10 Sandwich the layers with frosting, then spread on the top and side.

Devil's Food Cake with Orange Frosting

SERVES 8–10

2 oz (55 g) unsweetened cocoa powder

6 fl oz (175 ml) boiling water

6 oz (170 g) butter, at room temperature

12 oz (350 g) dark brown sugar

3 eggs, at room temperature

10 oz (285 g) plain flour

1½ teaspoons bicarbonate of soda

¼ teaspoon baking powder

4 fl oz (125 ml) soured cream

orange rind strips, for decoration

FOR THE FROSTING

10½ oz (300 g) caster sugar

2 egg whites

4 tablespoons frozen orange juice concentrate

1 tablespoon lemon juice

grated rind of 1 orange

1 Preheat a 350°F/180°C/Gas 4 oven. Line 2 9 in (23 cm) cake tins with greaseproof paper and grease. In a bowl, mix the cocoa and water until smooth. Set aside.

2 With an electric mixer, cream the butter and sugar until light and fluffy. Add the eggs, 1 at a time, beating well after each addition.

3 ▲ When the cocoa mixture is lukewarm, add to the butter mixture.

4 ▼ Sift together the flour, soda and baking powder twice. Fold into the cocoa mixture in 3 batches, alternating with the soured cream.

5 Pour into the tins and bake until the cakes pull away from the sides of the tins, 30–35 minutes. Let stand 15 minutes. Turn out onto a rack.

6 Thinly slice the orange rind strips. Blanch in boiling water for 1 minute.

7 ▲ For the frosting, place all the ingredients in the top of a double boiler or in a bowl set over hot water. With an electric mixer, beat until the mixture holds soft peaks. Continue beating off the heat until thick enough to spread.

8 Sandwich the cake layers with frosting, then spread over the top and side. Arrange the blanched orange rind strips on top of the cake.

Best-Ever Chocolate Sandwich

SERVES 12–14

4 oz (115 g) unsalted butter
4 oz (115 g) plain flour
2 oz (55 g) cocoa powder
1 tsp baking powder
⅛ tsp salt
6 eggs
8 oz (225 g) caster sugar
2 tsp vanilla essence
FOR THE ICING
8 oz (225 g) plain chocolate, chopped
3 oz (85 g) unsalted butter
3 eggs, separated
8 fl oz (250 ml) whipping cream
3 tbsp caster sugar

1 Preheat a 350°F/180°C/Gas 4 oven. Line 3 8 × 1½ in (20 × 3 cm) round tins with greaseproof paper and grease.

2 ▲ Dust evenly with flour and spread with a brush. Set aside.

~ **VARIATION** ~

For a simpler icing, combine 8 fl oz (250 ml) whipping cream with 8 oz (225 g) finely chopped plain chocolate in a saucepan. Stir over a low heat until the chocolate has melted. Cool and whisk to spreading consistency.

3 ▲ Melt the butter over a low heat. With a spoon, skim off any foam that rises to the surface. Set aside.

4 ▲ Sift the flour, cocoa, baking powder and salt together 3 times and set aside.

5 Place the eggs and sugar in a large heatproof bowl set over a pan of hot water. With an electric mixer, beat until the mixture doubles in volume and is thick enough to leave a ribbon trail when the beaters are lifted, about 10 minutes. Add the vanilla.

6 ▲ Sift over the dry ingredients in 3 batches, folding in carefully after each addition. Fold in the butter.

7 Divide the mixture between the tins and bake until the cakes pull away from the sides of the tin, about 25 minutes. Transfer to a rack.

8 For the icing, melt the chopped chocolate in the top of a double boiler, or in a heatproof bowl set over hot water.

9 ▲ Off the heat, stir in the butter and egg yolks. Return to a low heat and stir until thick. Remove from the heat and set aside.

10 Whip the cream until firm; set aside. In another bowl, beat the egg whites until stiff. Add the sugar and beat until glossy.

11 Fold the cream into the chocolate mixture, then carefully fold in the egg whites. Refrigerate for 20 minutes to thicken the icing.

12 ▲ Sandwich the cake layers with icing, stacking them carefully. Spread the remaining icing evenly over the top and sides of the cake.

Rich Chocolate Nut Cake

SERVES 10

8 oz (225 g) butter
8 oz (225 g) plain chocolate
4 oz (115 g) cocoa powder
12 oz (350 g) caster sugar
6 eggs
3 fl oz (85 ml) brandy or cognac
8 oz (225 g) finely chopped hazelnuts

FOR THE GLAZE

2 oz (55 g) butter
5 oz (140 g) bitter cooking chocolate
2 tbsp milk
1 tsp vanilla essence

1 Preheat a 350°F/180°C/Gas 4 oven. Line a 9 × 2 in (23 × 5 cm) round tin with greaseproof paper and grease.

2 Melt the butter and chocolate together in the top of a double boiler, or in a heatproof bowl set over hot water. Set aside to cool.

3 ▼ Sift the cocoa into a bowl. Add the sugar and eggs and stir until just combined. Pour in the melted chocolate mixture and brandy.

4 Fold in three-quarters of the nuts, then pour the mixture into the prepared tin.

5 ▲ Set the tin inside a large tin and pour 1 in (2.5 cm) of hot water into the outer tin. Bake until the cake is firm to the touch, about 45 minutes. Let stand 15 minutes, then unmould and transfer to a cooling rack.

6 Wrap the cake in greaseproof paper and refrigerate for 6 hours.

7 For the glaze, combine the butter, chocolate, milk and vanilla in the top of a double boiler or in a heatproof bowl set over hot water, until melted.

8 Place a piece of greaseproof paper under the cake, then drizzle spoonfuls of glaze along the edge to drip down and coat the sides. Pour the remaining glaze on top of the cake.

9 ▲ Cover the sides of the cake with the remaining nuts, gently pressing them on with the palm of your hand.

Chocolate Layer Cake

SERVES 8–10

4 oz (115 g) plain chocolate
6 oz (170 g) butter
1 lb (450 g) caster sugar
3 eggs
1 tsp vanilla essence
6 oz (170 g) plain flour
1 tsp baking powder
4 oz (115 g) chopped walnuts
FOR THE TOPPING
12 fl oz (350 ml) whipping cream
8 oz (225 g) plain chocolate
1 tbsp vegetable oil

1 Preheat a 350°F/180°C/Gas 4 oven. Line 2 8 in (20 cm) cake tins with greaseproof paper and grease.

2 Melt the chocolate and butter together in the top of a double boiler, or in a heatproof bowl set over a saucepan of hot water.

3 ▲ Transfer to a mixing bowl and stir in the sugar. Add the eggs and vanilla and mix until well blended.

~ **VARIATION** ~

To make Chocolate Ice Cream Layer Cake, sandwich the cake layers with softened vanilla ice cream. Freeze before serving.

4 ▲ Sift over the flour and baking powder. Stir in the walnuts.

5 Divide the mixture between the prepared tins and spread level.

6 Bake until a skewer inserted in the centre comes out clean, about 30 minutes. Let stand 10 minutes, then unmould and transfer to a rack.

7 When the cakes are cool, whip the cream until firm. With a long serrated knife, carefully slice each cake in half horizontally.

8 Sandwich the layers with some of the whipped cream and spread the remainder over the top and sides of the cake. Refrigerate until needed.

9 ▼ For the chocolate curls, melt the chocolate and oil in the top of a double boiler or a bowl set over hot water. Transfer to a non-porous surface. Spread to a ³⁄₈ in (1 cm) thick rectangle. Just before the chocolate sets, hold the blade of a straight knife at an angle to the chocolate and scrape across the surface to make curls. Place on top of the cake.

Sachertorte

SERVES 8–10

4 oz (115 g) plain chocolate
3 oz (85 g) unsalted butter, at room temperature
2 oz (55 g) sugar
4 eggs, separated
1 extra egg white
¼ teaspoon salt
2½ oz (70 g) plain flour, sifted

FOR THE TOPPING

5 tablespoons apricot jam
8 fl oz (250 ml) plus 1 tablespoon water
½ oz (15 g) unsalted butter
6 oz (170 g) plain chocolate
3 oz (85 g) sugar
ready-made chocolate decorating icing (optional)

1 Preheat the oven to 325°F/170°C/ Gas 3. Line a 9 × 2 in (23 × 5 cm) cake tin with greaseproof paper and grease.

2 ▲ Melt the chocolate in the top of a double boiler, or in a heatproof bowl set over hot water. Set aside.

3 With an electric mixer, cream the butter and sugar until light and fluffy. Stir in the chocolate.

4 ▲ Beat in the yolks, 1 at a time.

5 In another bowl, beat the egg whites with the salt until stiff.

6 ▲ Fold a dollop of whites into the chocolate mixture to lighten it. Fold in the remaining whites in 3 batches, alternating with the sifted flour.

7 ▲ Pour into the tin and bake until a cake tester comes out clean, about 45 minutes. Turn out onto a rack.

8 ▲ Meanwhile, melt the jam with 1 tablespoon of the water over low heat, then strain for a smooth consistency.

9 For the frosting, melt the butter and chocolate in the top of a double boiler or a bowl set over hot water.

10 ▲ In a heavy saucepan, dissolve the sugar in the remaining water over low heat. Raise the heat and boil until it reaches 225°F/107°C (thread stage) on a sugar thermometer. Immediately plunge the bottom of the pan into cold water for 1 minute. Pour into the chocolate mixture and stir to blend. Let cool for a few minutes.

11 To assemble, brush the warm jam over the cake. Starting in the centre, pour over the frosting and work outward in a circular movement. Tilt the rack to spread; use a palette knife to smooth the side of the cake. Leave to set overnight. If wished, decorate with chocolate icing.

Raspberry-Hazelnut Meringue Cake

SERVES 8

5 oz (140 g) hazelnuts
4 egg whites
⅛ teaspoon salt
7 oz (200 g) sugar
½ teaspoon vanilla essence
FOR THE FILLING
10 fl oz (300 ml) whipping cream
1 lb 8 oz (700 g) raspberries

1 Preheat a 350°F/180°C/Gas 4 oven. Line the bottom of 2 8 in (20 cm) cake tins with greaseproof paper and grease.

2 Spread the hazelnuts on a baking sheet and bake until lightly toasted, about 8 minutes. Let cool slightly.

3 ▲ Rub the hazelnuts vigorously in a clean tea towel to remove most of the skins.

4 Grind the nuts in a food processor, blender, or coffee grinder until they are the consistency of coarse sand.

5 Reduce oven to 300°F/150°C/Gas 2.

6 With an electric mixer, beat the egg whites and salt until they hold stiff peaks. Beat in 2 tablespoons of the sugar, then fold in the remaining sugar, a few tablespoons at a time, with a rubber scraper. Fold in the vanilla and the hazelnuts.

7 ▲ Divide the batter between the prepared tins and spread level.

8 Bake for 1¼ hours. If the meringues brown too quickly, protect with a sheet of foil. Let stand 5 minutes, then carefully run a knife around the inside edge of the tins to loosen. Turn out onto a rack to cool.

9 For the filling, whip the cream just until firm.

10 ▲ Spread half the cream in an even layer on one meringue round and top with half the raspberries.

11 Top with the other meringue round. Spread the remaining cream on top and arrange the remaining raspberries over the cream. Refrigerate for 1 hour to facilitate cutting.

Forgotten Gâteau

SERVES 6

6 egg whites, at room temperature
½ teaspoon cream of tartar
⅛ teaspoon salt
10½ oz (300 g) caster sugar
1 teaspoon vanilla essence
6 fl oz (175 ml) whipping cream
FOR THE SAUCE
12 oz (350 g) fresh or thawed frozen raspberries
2–3 tablespoons icing sugar

1 Preheat a 450°F/230°C/Gas 8 oven. Grease a 2⅓ pt (1.5 litre) ring mould.

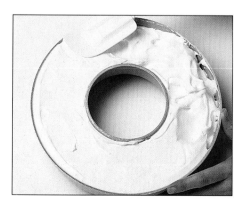

2 ▲ With an electric mixer, beat the egg whites, cream of tartar and salt until they hold soft peaks. Gradually add the sugar and beat until glossy and stiff. Fold in the vanilla.

3 ▲ Spoon into the prepared mould and smooth the top level.

4 Place in the oven, then turn the oven off. Leave overnight; do not open the oven door at any time.

5 ▼ To serve, gently loosen the edge with a sharp knife and turn out onto a serving plate. Whip the cream until firm. Spread it over the top and upper sides of the meringue and decorate with any meringue crumbs.

6 ▲ For the sauce, purée the fruit, then strain. Sweeten to taste.

~ COOK'S TIP ~

This recipe is not suitable for fan-assisted and solid fuel ovens.

Nut and Apple Gâteau

SERVES 8

4 oz (115 g) pecan nuts or walnuts

2 oz (55 g) plain flour

2 tsp baking powder

¼ tsp salt

2 large cooking apples

3 eggs

8 oz (225 g) caster sugar

1 tsp vanilla essence

6 fl oz (175 ml) whipping cream

1 Preheat a 325°F/170°C/Gas 3 oven. Line 2 9 in (23 cm) cake tins with greaseproof paper and grease the paper. Spread the nuts on a baking sheet and bake for 10 minutes.

2 Finely chop the nuts. Reserve 1½ tablespoons and place the rest in a mixing bowl. Sift over the flour, baking powder and salt and stir.

3 ▲ Quarter, core and peel the apples. Cut into ⅛ in (3 mm) dice, then stir into the nut-flour mixture.

4 ▲ With an electric mixer, beat the eggs until frothy. Gradually add the sugar and vanilla and beat until a ribbon forms, about 8 minutes. Gently fold in the flour mixture.

5 Pour into the tins and level the tops. Bake until a skewer inserted in the centre comes out clean, about 35 minutes. Let stand 10 minutes.

6 ▲ To loosen, run a knife around the inside edge of each layer. Let cool.

7 ▲ Whip the cream until firm. Spread half over the cake. Top with the second cake. Pipe whipped cream rosettes on top and sprinkle over the reserved nuts before serving.

Almond Cake

SERVES 4–6

8 oz (225 g) blanched whole almonds, plus more for decorating
1 oz (30 g) butter
3 oz (85 g) icing sugar
3 eggs
½ tsp almond essence
1 oz (30 g) plain flour
3 egg whites
1 tbsp caster sugar

1 ▲ Preheat a 325°F/170°C/Gas 3 oven. Line a 9 in (23 cm) round cake tin with greaseproof paper and grease.

2 ▲ Spread the almonds in a baking tray and toast for 10 minutes. Cool, then coarsely chop 8 oz (225 g).

3 Melt the butter and set aside.

4 Preheat a 400°F/200°C/Gas 6 oven.

5 Grind the chopped almonds with half the icing sugar in a food processor, blender or grinder. Transfer to a mixing bowl.

6 ▲ Add the whole eggs and remaining icing sugar. With an electric mixer, beat until the mixture forms a ribbon when the beaters are lifted. Mix in the butter and almond essence. Sift over the flour and fold in gently.

7 With an electric mixer, beat the egg whites until they hold soft peaks. Add the caster sugar and beat until stiff and glossy.

8 ▲ Fold the whites into the almond mixture in 4 batches.

9 Spoon the mixture into the prepared tin and bake in the centre of the oven until golden brown, about 15–20 minutes. Decorate the top with the remaining toasted whole almonds. Serve warm.

Walnut Coffee Gâteau

SERVES 8–10

5 oz (140 g) walnuts
5½ oz (150 g) sugar
5 eggs, separated
2 oz (55 g) dry breadcrumbs
1 tablespoon unsweetened cocoa powder
1 tablespoon instant coffee
2 tablespoons rum or lemon juice
⅛ teaspoon salt
6 tablespoons redcurrant jelly
chopped walnuts, for decorating
FOR THE FROSTING
8 oz (225 g) plain chocolate
1¼ pt (750 ml) whipping cream

1 ▲ For the frosting, combine the chocolate and cream in the top of a double boiler, or in a heatproof bowl set over simmering water. Stir until the chocolate melts. Let cool, then cover and refrigerate overnight or until the mixture is firm.

2 Preheat the oven to 350°F/180°C/ Gas 4. Line a 9 × 2 in (23 × 5 cm) cake tin with greaseproof paper and grease.

3 ▲ Grind the nuts with 3 tablespoons of the sugar in a food processor, blender, or coffee grinder.

4 With an electric mixer, beat the egg yolks and remaining sugar until thick and lemon-coloured.

5 ▲ Fold in the walnuts. Stir in the breadcrumbs, cocoa, coffee and rum or lemon juice.

6 ▲ In another bowl, beat the egg whites with the salt until they hold stiff peaks. Fold carefully into the walnut mixture with a rubber scraper.

7 Pour the meringue batter into the prepared tin and bake until the top of the cake springs back when touched lightly, about 45 minutes. Let the cake stand for 5 minutes, then turn out and cool on a rack.

8 ▲ When cool, slice the cake in half horizontally.

9 With an electric mixer, beat the chocolate frosting mixture on low speed until it becomes lighter, about 30 seconds. Do not overbeat or it may become grainy.

10 ▲ Warm the jelly in a saucepan until melted, then brush over the cut cake layer. Spread with some of the chocolate frosting, then sandwich with the remaining cake layer. Brush the top of the cake with jelly, then cover the side and top with the remaining chocolate frosting. Make a starburst pattern by pressing gently with a table knife in lines radiating from the centre. Sprinkle the chopped walnuts around the edge.

Light Fruit Cake

MAKES 2 LOAVES

8 oz (225 g) prunes
8 oz (225 g) dates
8 oz (225 g) currants
8 oz (225 g) sultanas
8 fl oz (250 ml) dry white wine
8 fl oz (250 ml) rum
12 oz (350 g) plain flour
2 tsp baking powder
1 tsp ground cinnamon
½ tsp grated nutmeg
8 oz (225 g) butter, at room temperature
8 oz (225 g) caster sugar
4 eggs, at room temperature, lightly beaten
1 tsp vanilla essence

1 Stone the prunes and dates and chop finely. Place in a bowl with the currants and sultanas.

2 ▲ Stir in the wine and rum and let stand, covered, for 48 hours. Stir occasionally.

3 Preheat a 300°F/150°C/Gas 2 oven with a tray of hot water in the bottom. Line 2 9 × 5 in (23 × 13 cm) tins with greaseproof paper and grease.

4 Sift together the flour, baking powder, cinnamon, and nutmeg.

5 ▲ With an electric mixer, cream the butter and sugar together until light and fluffy.

6 Gradually add the eggs and vanilla. Fold in the flour mixture in 3 batches. Fold in the dried fruit mixture and its soaking liquid.

7 ▲ Divide the mixture between the tins and bake until a skewer inserted in the centre comes out clean, about 1½ hours.

8 Let stand 20 minutes, then unmould and transfer to a cooling rack. Wrap in foil and store in an airtight container. If possible, leave for at least 1 week before serving to allow the flavours to mellow.

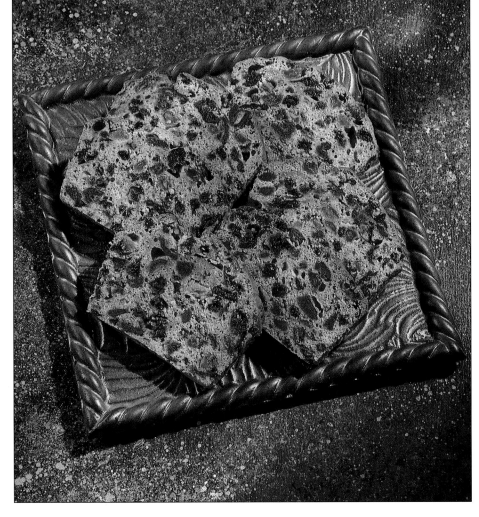

Rich Fruit Cake

SERVES 12

5 oz (140 g) currants
6 oz (170 g) raisins
2 oz (55 g) sultanas
2 oz (55 g) glacé cherries, halved
3 tbsp sweet sherry
6 oz (170 g) butter
7 oz (200 g) dark brown sugar
2 size 1 eggs, at room temperature
7 oz (200 g) plain flour
2 tsp baking powder
2 tsp each ground ginger, allspice, and cinnamon
1 tbsp golden syrup
1 tbsp milk
2 oz (55 g) cut mixed peel
4 oz (115 g) chopped walnuts

FOR THE DECORATION

8 oz (225 g) caster sugar
4 fl oz (125 ml) water
1 lemon, thinly sliced
½ orange, thinly sliced
4 fl oz (125 ml) orange marmalade
glacé cherries

1 One day before preparing, combine the currants, raisins, sultanas and cherries in a bowl. Stir in the sherry. Cover and let stand overnight to soak.

2 Preheat a 300°F/150°C/Gas 2 oven. Line a 9 × 3 in (23 × 8 cm) springform tin with greaseproof paper and grease. Place a tray of hot water on the bottom of the oven.

3 With an electric mixer, cream the butter and sugar until light and fluffy. Beat in the eggs, 1 at a time.

4 ▲ Sift the flour, baking powder and spices together 3 times. Fold into the butter mixture in 3 batches. Fold in the syrup, milk, dried fruit and liquid, mixed peel and nuts.

5 ▲ Spoon into the tin, spreading out so there is a slight depression in the centre of the mixture.

6 Bake until a skewer inserted in the centre comes out clean, 2½–3 hours. Cover with foil when the top is golden to prevent over-browning. Cool in the tin on a rack.

7 ▲ For the decoration, combine the sugar and water in a saucepan and bring to the boil. Add the lemon and orange slices and cook until crystallized, about 20 minutes. Work in batches, if necessary. Remove the fruit with a slotted spoon. Pour the remaining syrup over the cake and let cool. Melt the marmalade over low heat, then brush over the top of the cake. Decorate with the crystallized citrus slices and cherries.

Whiskey Cake

MAKES 1 LOAF

6 oz (170 g) chopped walnuts
3 oz (85 g) raisins, chopped
3 oz (85 g) currants
4 oz (115 g) plain flour
1 tsp baking powder
¼ tsp salt
4 oz (115 g) butter
8 oz (225 g) caster sugar
3 eggs, at room temperature, separated
1 tsp grated nutmeg
½ tsp ground cinnamon
3 fl oz (85 ml) Irish whiskey or bourbon
icing sugar, for dusting

1 ▼ Preheat a 325°F/170°C/Gas 3 oven. Line a 9 × 5 in (23 × 13 cm) loaf tin with greaseproof paper. Grease the paper and sides of the pan.

2 ▲ Place the walnuts, raisins, and currants in a bowl. Sprinkle over 2 tablespoons of the flour, mix and set aside. Sift together the remaining flour, baking powder and salt.

3 ▲ Cream the butter and sugar until light and fluffy. Beat in the egg yolks.

4 Mix the nutmeg, cinnamon and whiskey. Fold into the butter mixture, alternating with the flour mixture.

5 ▲ In another bowl, beat the egg whites until stiff. Fold into the whiskey mixture until just blended. Fold in the walnut mixture.

6 Bake until a skewer inserted in the centre comes out clean, about 1 hour. Let cool in the pan. Dust with icing sugar over a template.

Gingerbread

SERVES 8–10

1 tbsp vinegar
6 fl oz (175 ml) milk
6 oz (170 g) plain flour
2 tsp baking powder
¼ tsp bicarbonate of soda
½ tsp salt
2 tsp ground ginger
1 tsp ground cinnamon
¼ tsp ground cloves
4 oz (115 g) butter, at room temperature
4 oz (115 g) caster sugar
1 egg, at room temperature
6 fl oz (175 ml) black treacle
whipped cream, for serving
chopped stem ginger, for decorating

1 ▲ Preheat a 350°F/180°C/Gas 4 oven. Line an 8 in (20 cm) square cake tin with greaseproof paper and grease the paper and the sides of the pan.

2 ▲ Add the vinegar to the milk and set aside. It will curdle.

3 In another mixing bowl, sift all the dry ingredients together 3 times and set aside.

4 With an electric mixer, cream the butter and sugar until light and fluffy. Beat in the egg until well combined.

5 ▼ Stir in the black treacle.

6 ▲ Fold in the dry ingredients in 4 batches, alternating with the curdled milk. Mix only enough to blend.

7 Pour into the prepared tin and bake until firm, 45–50 minutes. Cut into squares and serve warm, with whipped cream. Decorate with the stem ginger.

Classic Cheesecake

SERVES 8

2 oz (55 g) digestive biscuits, crushed

2 lb (900 g) cream cheese, at room temperature

8¾ oz (240 g) sugar

grated rind of 1 lemon

3 tablespoons lemon juice

1 teapoon vanilla essence

4 eggs, at room temperature

1 Preheat the oven to 325°F/170°C/ Gas 3. Grease an 8 in (20 cm) springform tin. Place on a round of foil 4–5 in (10–12.5 cm) larger than the diameter of the tin. Press it up the sides to seal tightly.

2 Sprinkle the crushed biscuits in the base of the tin. Press to form an even layer.

3 With an electric mixer, beat the cream cheese until smooth. Add the sugar, lemon rind and juice, and vanilla, and beat until blended. Beat in the eggs, 1 at a time. Beat just enough to blend thoroughly.

4 ▲ Pour into the prepared tin. Set the tin in a larger baking tray and place in the oven. Pour enough hot water in the outer tray to come 1 in (2.5 cm) up the side of the tin.

5 Bake until the top of the cake is golden brown, about 1½ hours. Let cool in the tin.

6 ▼ Run a knife around the edge to loosen, then remove the rim of the tin. Refrigerate for at least 4 hours before serving.

Chocolate Cheesecake

SERVES 10–12

10 oz (285 g) plain chocolate

2 lb 8 oz (1.2 kg) cream cheese, at room temperature

7 oz (200 g) sugar

2 teaspoons vanilla essence

4 eggs, at room temperature

6 fl oz (175 ml) soured cream

1 tablespoon cocoa powder

FOR THE BASE

7 oz (200 g) chocolate biscuits, crushed

3 oz (85 g) butter, melted

½ teaspoon ground cinnamon

1 Preheat a 350°F/180°C/Gas 4 oven. Grease the bottom and sides of a 9 × 3 in (23 × 7.5 cm) springform tin.

2 ▲ For the base, mix the crushed biscuits with the butter and cinnamon. Press evenly onto the bottom of the tin.

3 Melt the chocolate in the top of a double boiler, or in a heatproof bowl set over hot water. Set aside.

4 Beat the cream cheese until smooth, then beat in the sugar and vanilla. Add the eggs, 1 at a time.

5 Stir the soured cream into the cocoa powder to form a paste. Add to the cream cheese mixture. Stir in the melted chocolate.

6 ▼ Pour into the crust. Bake for 1 hour. Let cool in the tin; remove rim. Refrigerate before serving.

Classic Cheesecake (top), Chocolate Cheesecake

Lemon Mousse Cheesecake

SERVES 10–12

2½ lb (1.2 kg) cream cheese, at room temperature
12 oz (350 g) caster sugar
1½ oz (45 g) plain flour
4 eggs, at room temperature, separated
4 fl oz (125 ml) fresh lemon juice
grated rind of 2 lemons
4 oz (115 g) digestive biscuits, crushed

1 Preheat a 325°F/170°C/Gas 3 oven. Line a 10 × 2 in (25 × 5 cm) round cake tin with greaseproof paper and grease the paper.

2 With an electric mixer, beat the cream cheese until smooth. Gradually add 10 oz (285 g) of the sugar, and beat until light. Beat in the flour.

3 ▲ Add the egg yolks, and lemon juice and rind, and beat until smooth and well blended.

4 In another bowl, beat the egg whites until they hold soft peaks. Add the remaining sugar and beat until stiff and glossy.

5 ▲ Add the egg whites to the cheese mixture and gently fold in.

6 Pour the mixture into the prepared tin, then place the tin in a larger baking tin. Place in the oven and pour hot water in the outer tin to come 1 in (2.5 cm) up the side.

7 Bake until golden, 60–65 minutes. Let cool in the pan on a rack. Cover and refrigerate for at least 4 hours.

8 To unmould, run a knife around the inside edge. Place a flat plate, bottom-side up, over the pan and invert onto the plate. Smooth the top with a metal spatula.

9 ▲ Sprinkle the biscuits over the top in an even layer, pressing down slightly to make a top crust.

10 To serve, cut slices with a sharp knife dipped in hot water.

Marbled Cheesecake

SERVES 10

2 oz (55 g) unsweetened cocoa powder

5 tablespoons hot water

2 lb (900 g) cream cheese, at room temperature

7 oz (200 g) sugar

4 eggs

1 teaspoon vanilla essence

2½ oz (70 g) digestive biscuits, crushed

1 Preheat a 350°F/180°C/Gas 4 oven. Line an 8 × 3 in (20 × 8 cm) cake tin with greaseproof paper and grease.

2 Sift the cocoa powder into a bowl. Pour over the hot water and stir to dissolve. Set aside.

3 With an electric mixer, beat the cheese until smooth and creamy. Add the sugar and beat to incorporate. Beat in the eggs, one at a time. Do not overmix.

4 Divide the mixture evenly between 2 bowls. Stir the chocolate mixture into one, then add the vanilla to the remaining mixture.

5 ▲ Pour a cupful of the plain mixture into the centre of the tin; it will spread out into an even layer. Slowly pour over a cupful of chocolate mixture in the centre.

6 ▲ Repeat alternating cupfuls of the batters in a circular pattern until both are used up.

7 Set the tin in a larger baking tray and pour in hot water to come 1½ in (3 cm) up the sides of the cake tin.

8 Bake until the top of the cake is golden, about 1½ hours. It will rise during baking but will sink later. Let cool in the tin on a rack.

9 To turn out, run a knife around the inside edge. Place a flat plate, bottom-side up, over the tin and invert onto the plate.

10 ▼ Sprinkle the crushed biscuits evenly over the base, gently place another plate over them, and invert again. Cover and refrigerate for at least 3 hours, or overnight. To serve, cut slices with a sharp knife dipped in hot water.

Heart Cake

MAKES 1 CAKE

8 oz (225 g) butter or margarine, at room temperature
8 oz (225 g) caster sugar
4 eggs, at room temperature
6 oz (170 g) plain flour
1 tsp baking powder
½ tsp bicarbonate of soda
2 tbsp milk
1 tsp vanilla essence
FOR ICING AND DECORATING
3 egg whites
12 oz (350 g) caster sugar
2 tbsp cold water
2 tbsp fresh lemon juice
¼ tsp cream of tartar
pink food colouring
3–4 oz (85–115 g) icing sugar

1 Preheat a 350°F/180°C/Gas 4 oven. Line an 8 in (20 cm) heart-shaped tin with greaseproof paper and grease.

2 ▲ With an electric mixer, cream the butter or margarine and sugar until light and fluffy. Add the eggs, 1 at a time, beating thoroughly after each addition.

3 Sift the flour, baking powder and baking soda together. Fold the dry ingredients into the butter mixture in 3 batches, alternating with the milk. Stir in the vanilla.

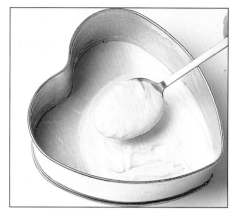

4 ▲ Spoon the mixture into the prepared tin and bake until a skewer inserted in the centre comes out clean, 35–40 minutes. Let the cake stand in the tin for 5 minutes, then unmould and transfer to a rack to cool completely.

5 For the icing, combine 2 of the egg whites, the caster sugar, water, lemon juice and cream of tartar in the top of a double boiler or in a bowl set over simmering water. With an electric mixer, beat until thick and holding soft peaks, about 7 minutes. Remove from the heat and continue beating until the mixture is thick enough to spread. Tint the icing with the pink food colouring.

6 ▲ Put the cake on a board, about 12 in (30 cm) square, covered in foil or in paper suitable for contact with food. Spread the icing evenly on the cake. Smooth the top and sides. Leave to set for 3–4 hours, or overnight.

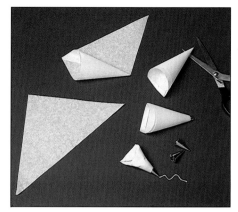

7 ▲ For the paper piping bags, fold an 11 × 8 in (28 × 20 cm) sheet of greaseproof paper in half diagonally, then cut into 2 pieces along the fold mark. Roll over the short side, so that it meets the right-angled corner and forms a cone. To form the piping bag, hold the cone in place with one hand, wrap the point of the long side of the triangle around the cone, and tuck inside, folding over twice to secure. Snip a hole in the pointed end and slip in a small metal piping nozzle to extend about ¼ in (5 mm).

8 For the piped decorations, place 1 tablespoon of the remaining egg white in a bowl and whisk until frothy. Gradually beat in enough icing sugar to make a stiff mixture suitable for piping.

9 ▲ Spoon into a paper piping bag to half-fill. Fold over the top and squeeze to pipe decorations on the top and sides of the cake.

Iced Fancies

MAKES 16

4 oz (115 g) butter, at room temperature
8 oz (225 g) caster sugar
2 eggs, at room temperature
6 oz (170 g) plain flour
¼ tsp salt
1½ tsp baking powder
4 fl oz (125 ml) plus 1 tbsp milk
1 tsp vanilla essence
FOR ICING AND DECORATING
2 large egg whites
14 oz (400 g) sifted icing sugar
1–2 drops glycerine
juice of 1 lemon
food colourings
hundreds and thousands, for decorating
crystallized lemon and orange slices, for decorating

1 Preheat a 375°F/190°C/Gas 5 oven.

2 ▲ Line 16 bun-tray cups with fluted paper baking cases, or grease.

~ COOK'S TIP ~

Ready-made cake decorating products are widely available, and may be used, if preferred, instead of the recipes given for icing and decorating. Coloured icing in ready-to-pipe tubes is useful.

3 With an electric mixer, cream the butter and sugar until light and fluffy. Add the eggs, 1 at a time, beating well after each addition.

4 Sift together the flour, salt and baking powder. Stir into the butter mixture, alternating with the milk. Stir in the vanilla.

5 ▲ Fill the cups half-full and bake until the tops spring back when touched lightly, about 20 minutes. Let the cakes stand in the tray for 5 minutes, then unmould and transfer to a rack to cool completely.

6 For the icing, beat the egg whites until stiff but not dry. Gradually add the sugar, glycerine and lemon juice, and continue beating for 1 minute. The consistency should be spreadable. If necessary, thin with a little water or add more sifted icing sugar.

7 ▲ Divide the icing between several bowls and tint with food colourings. Spread different coloured icings over the cooled cakes.

8 ▲ Decorate the cakes as wished, with sugar decorations such as hundreds and thousands.

9 ▲ Other decorations include crystallized orange and lemon slices. Cut into small pieces and arrange on top of the cakes. Alternatively, use other suitable sweets.

10 ▲ To make freehand iced decorations, fill paper piping bags with different colour icings. Pipe on faces, or make other designs.

Snake Cake

SERVES 10–12

8 oz (225 g) butter or margarine, at room temperature

grated rind and juice of 1 small orange

8 oz (225 g) sugar

4 eggs, at room temperature, separated

6 oz (170 g) plain flour

1 teaspoon baking powder

pinch of salt

FOR THE ICING AND DECORATING

1 oz (30 g) butter, at room temperature

12 oz (350 g) icing sugar

5 oz (140 g) plain chocolate

pinch of salt

4 fl oz (125 ml) soured cream

1 egg white

green and blue food colourings

1 Preheat the oven to 375°F/190°C/ Gas 5. Grease 2 8½ oz (22 cm) ring tins and dust them with flour.

2 Cream the butter or margarine, orange rind and sugar until light. Beat in the egg yolks, 1 at a time.

3 Sift the flour and baking powder. Fold into the butter mixture, alternating with the orange juice.

4 ▲ In another bowl, beat the egg whites and salt until stiff.

5 Fold a large dollop of the egg whites into the creamed butter mixture to lighten it, then gently fold in the remaining whites.

6 Divide the mixture between the prepared tins and bake until a skewer inserted in the centre comes out clean, about 25 minutes. Leave to stand for 5 minutes, then turn out on to a wire rack to cool.

7 Prepare a board, 24 x 8 in (60 x 20 cm), covered in paper suitable for contact with food, or in foil.

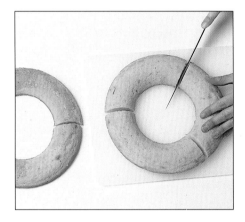

8 ▲ Cut the cakes into 3 even pieces. Trim to level the flat side, if necessary, and shape the head by cutting off wedges from the front. Shape the tail in the same way.

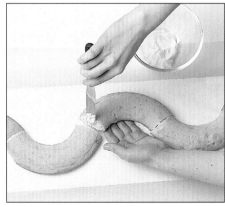

9 ▲ For the buttercream, mix the butter with 1½ oz (45 g) of the icing sugar. Use to join the cake sections and arrange on the board.

10 ▲ For the chocolate icing, melt the chocolate. Stir in the salt and soured cream. When cool, spread over the cake and smooth the surface.

11 ▲ For the decoration, beat the egg white until frothy. Add enough of the remaining icing sugar to obtain a thick mixture. Divide among several bowls and add food colourings.

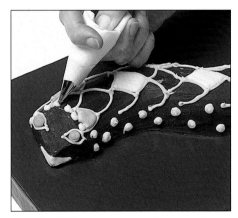

12 ▲ Fill paper piping bags with icing and pipe decorations along the top of the cake.

Sun Cake

SERVES 10–12

4 oz (115 g) unsalted butter
6 eggs
8 oz (225 g) caster sugar
4 oz (115 g) plain flour
½ tsp salt
1 tsp vanilla essence
FOR ICING AND DECORATING
1 oz (30 g) unsalted butter, at room temperature
1 lb (450 g) sifted icing sugar
4 fl oz (125 ml) apricot jam
2 tbsp water
2 large egg whites
1–2 drops glycerine
juice of 1 lemon
yellow and orange food colourings

1 Preheat a 350°F/180°C/Gas 4 oven. Line 2 8 × 2 in (20 × 5 cm) round cake tins, then grease and flour.

2 In a saucepan, melt the butter over very low heat. Skim off any foam that rises to the surface, then set aside.

3 ▲ Place a heatproof bowl over a saucepan of hot water. Add the eggs and sugar. Beat with an electric mixer until the mixture doubles in volume and is thick enough to leave a ribbon trail when the beaters are lifted, 8–10 minutes.

4 Sift the flour and salt together 3 times. Sift over the egg mixture in 3 batches, folding in well after each addition. Fold in the melted butter and vanilla.

5 Divide the mixture between the tins. Level the surfaces and bake until the cakes shrink slightly from the sides of the tins, 25–30 minutes. Let stand 5 minutes, then unmould and transfer to a cooling rack.

6 Prepare a board, 16 in (40 cm) square, covered in paper suitable for contact with food, or in foil.

7 ▲ For the sunbeams, cut one of the cakes into 8 equal wedges. Cut away a rounded piece from the base of each so that they fit neatly up against the sides of the whole cake.

8 ▲ For the butter icing, mix the butter and 1 oz (30 g) of the icing sugar. Use to attach the sunbeams.

9 ▲ Melt the jam with the water and brush over the cake. Place on the board and straighten, if necessary.

10 ▲ For the icing, beat the egg whites until stiff but not dry. Gradually add 14 oz (400 g) icing sugar, the glycerine and lemon juice, and continue beating for 1 minute. If necessary, thin with water or add a little more sugar. Tint with yellow food colouring and spread over the cake.

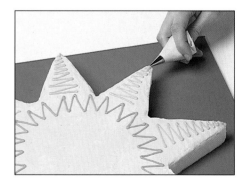

11 ▲ Divide the remaining icing in half and tint with more food colouring to obtain bright yellow and orange. Pipe decorative zigzags on the sunbeams and a face in the middle.

Jack-O'-Lantern Cake

SERVES 8–10

6 oz (170 g) plain flour
2½ teaspoons baking powder
pinch of salt
4 oz (115 g) butter, at room temperature
8 oz (225 g) sugar
3 egg yolks, at room temperature, well beaten
1 teaspoon grated lemon rind
6 fl oz (175 ml) milk
FOR THE CAKE COVERING
1 lb 4 oz–1 lb 8 oz (565–700 g) icing sugar
2 egg whites
2 tablespoons liquid glucose
orange and black food colourings

1 Preheat the oven to 375°F/190°C/ Gas 5. Line an 8 in (20 cm) round cake tin with greaseproof paper and grease.

2 Sift together the flour, baking powder and salt. Set aside.

3 With an electric mixer, cream the butter and sugar until light and fluffy. Gradually beat in the egg yolks, then add the lemon rind. Fold in the flour mixture in 3 batches, alternating with the milk.

4 Spoon the mixture into the prepared tin. Bake until a skewer inserted in the centre comes out clean, about 35 minutes. Leave to stand, then turn out on to a rack.

> ~ **COOK'S TIP** ~
>
> If preferred, use ready-made roll-out cake covering, available at cake decorating supply shops. Knead in food colouring, if required.

5 For the icing, sift 1 lb 4 oz (565 g) of the icing sugar into a bowl. Make a well in the centre, add 1 egg white, the glucose and orange food colouring. Stir until a dough forms.

6 ▲ Transfer to a clean work surface dusted with icing sugar and knead briefly.

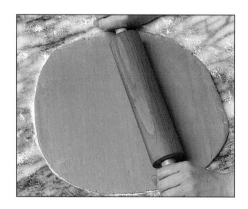

7 ▲ Carefully roll out the orange cake covering to a thin sheet.

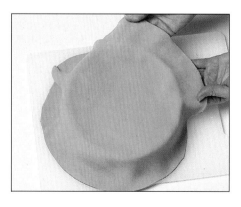

8 ▲ Place the sheet on top of the cooled cake and smooth the sides. Trim the excess icing and reserve.

9 ▲ From the trimmings, cut shapes for the top. Tint the remaining cake covering trimmings with black food colouring. Roll out thinly and cut shapes for the face.

10 ▲ Brush the undersides with water and arrange the face on top of the cake.

11 ▲ Place 1 tablespoon of the remaining egg white in a bowl and stir in enough icing sugar to make a thick icing. Tint with black food colouring, fill a paper piping bag and complete the decoration.

Stars and Stripes Cake

SERVES 20

8 oz (225 g) butter or margarine, at room temperature

8 oz (225 g) dark brown sugar

8 oz (225 g) granulated sugar

5 eggs, at room temperature

10 oz (285 g) plain flour

2 teaspoons baking powder

1 teaspoon bicarbonate of soda

1 teaspoon ground cinnamon

1 teaspoon ground ginger

½ teaspoon ground allspice

¼ teaspoon ground cloves

¼ teaspoon salt

12 fl oz (350 ml) buttermilk

3 oz (85 g) raisins

FOR THE CAKE COVERING

1 oz (30 g) butter

2 lb 4 oz–2 lb 10 oz (1–1.3 kg) icing sugar

3 egg whites

4 tablespoons liquid glucose

red and blue food colourings

1 Preheat the oven to 350°F/180°C/ Gas 4. Line a 12 x 9 in (30 x 23 cm) baking tin with greaseproof paper and lightly grease.

2 With an electric mixer, cream the butter or margarine and sugars until light and fluffy. Gradually beat in the eggs, 1 at a time, beating well after each addition.

3 Sift together the flour, baking powder, bicarbonate of soda, spices and salt. Fold into the butter mixture in 3 batches, alternating with the buttermilk. Stir in the raisins.

4 Pour the mixture into the prepared tin and bake until the cake springs back when touched lightly, about 35 minutes. Leave to stand for 10 minutes, then turn out on to a wire rack.

5 Make buttercream for assembling the cake by mixing the butter with 1½ oz (45 g) of the icing sugar.

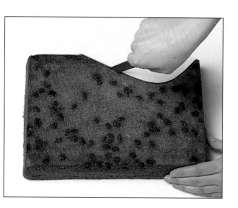

6 ▲ When the cake is cool, cut a curved shape from the top.

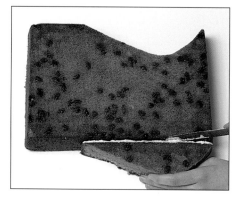

7 ▲ Attach it to the bottom of the cake with the buttercream.

8 Prepare a board, about 16 x 12 in (40 x 30 cm), covered in paper suitable for contact with food, or in foil. Transfer the cake to the board.

9 For the cake covering, sift 2 lb 4 oz (1 kg) of the icing sugar into a bowl. Add 2 of the egg whites and the liquid glucose. Stir until the mixture forms a dough.

10 Cover and set aside half of the covering. On a clean work surface lightly dusted with icing sugar, roll out the remaining covering to a sheet. Carefully transfer to the cake. Smooth the sides and trim any excess from the bottom edges.

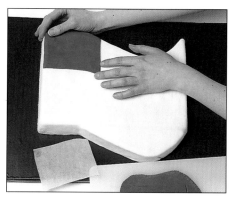

11 ▲ Tint one quarter of the remaining covering blue and tint the rest red. Roll out the blue to a thin sheet and cut out the background for the stars. Place on the cake.

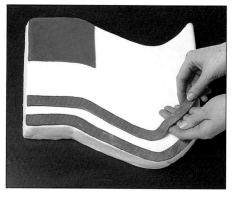

12 ▲ Roll out the red covering, cut out stripes and place on the cake.

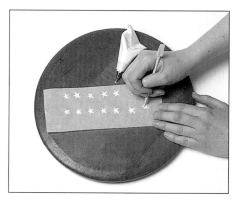

13 ▲ For the stars, mix 1 tablespoon of the egg white with just enough icing sugar to thicken. Pipe small stars on to a sheet of greaseproof paper and leave to set. When dry, peel them off and place on the blue background.

INDEX

~